THE MARVELOUS MADNESS OF MOTHERHOOD

Things No One Ever Told Me About Being a Mom!

REBECCA D. KEENER

Unless otherwise indicated, all Scripture quotations are taken from the *Holy Bible*, King James Authorized Version, which is in the public domain.

Scripture quotations marked NIV are taken from the *Holy Bible,* New International Version, copyright © 1973, 1978, 1984 International Bible Society. Used by permission of Zondervan, Grand Rapids, Michigan. Scripture quotations marked AMP are taken from the Amplified Bible, copyright © 1954, 1958, 1962, 1965, 1987. Used by permission of The Lockman Foundation, La Habra, California. Scripture quotations marked NKJV are taken from the *Holy Bible, New King James Version*, copyright ©1979, 1980, 1982. Used by permission of Thomas Nelson, Inc., Nashville, Tennessee.

THE MARVELOUS MADNESS OF MOTHERHOOD: Things No One Ever Told Me About Being a Mom!

ISBN 0-924748-74-5

UPC 885713000444

Printed in the United States of America

Milestones International Publishers
P.O. Box 104
Newburg, PA 17240
717-477-2230
303-503-7257
www.milestonesintl.com

1 2 3 4 5 6 7 8 9 10 11 / 12 11 10 09

ENDORSEMENTS

"This book has been long overdue—I've often thought someone should write a book to help mothers with the things no one told them, and there's no one better to do this than Rebecca Keener. I've watched the Keeners involve their children in all sorts of activities with great results. They are uniquely qualified to share these great insights with parents everywhere; every parent will love this book."

Tommy Barnett
Pastor, Phoenix First Assembly

"The madness this mother refers to is not madness at all. The Keeners are model parents who have transparently shared their journey and observations in a manner that is bound to help parents. This should be required reading for new parents, and a refresher course for those who find themselves in the busy years of parenting."

Dr. Leo Godzich
N.A.M.E. (National Association of Marriage Enhancement)
Author, *Men Are from Dirt, Women Are from Men*

"This book, *The Marvelous Madness of Motherhood,* is well needed today as so many mothers need help and direction. Thanks to Becky for her insight, reaching out to share with others who need a support system and an answer to the question, "How did you do it?" Readers, you will be blessed by this book. Enjoy!"

Deloris Jordan
Author, *Salt in His Shoes: Michael Jordan in Pursuit of a Dream*

"Becky is a truly remarkable speaker and I am personally thrilled to see her publish this book. Her combination of Godly wisdom, practical insight, and humor is wonderful. It is refreshing to see someone so down to earth and so willing to be transparent before God and man. She and her husband Edward are raising three delightful boys who I know will grow up to be tremendous men of God. I am certain that you will love this book about that marvelous madness we call motherhood!"

Debi Vandenboom
Founder of Women Unite

"Thoroughly qualified and uniquely gifted, Becky Keener gives a gold mine of Scriptural wisdom and practical advice in her new book, *The Marvelous Madness of Motherhood.* This book is a must-read for every parent who wants to raise champions for Christ."

Jentezen Franklin
Pastor, Free Chapel Worship Center, Gainesville, GA

Becky Keener is truly inspirational in her new book, *The Marvelous Madness of Motherhood.* Becky, herself an incredible wife and mother, has written this compelling book from firsthand experience. This book is a must-read for all mothers and those who desire to be one some day. Her lovely southern style and heartfelt wisdom will bless all those who desire to excel at the greatest job of all—motherhood!

Kristie Barnett Sexton
Pastor of Volunteerism
Founder of Phoenix Girls Women's Ministry
Phoenix First Assembly

ACKNOWLEDGEMENTS

To my husband Edward and sons Davis, Hamilton, and Truett—Thanks for all your encouragement, prayers, and support, for never letting me give up on my dream to write. Thanks most of all for the material you provided! I love you so!

To my parents, Dr. Terrell and Bernice Davis—You are oaks of righteousness! Thanks for EVERYTHING you did to make this book possible. You are incredible parents and friends. I love you!

To Cherise Franklin—Thanks for so many fun times together and for the conversation which sparked the idea for writing on motherhood. You are a beautiful mother and friend. And to Pastor Jentezen for years of incredible teaching and anointed words from God. You both are amazing.

To Audrey and Bob Meisner—Thanks for encouraging me in writing and for being used of God to open a great and effectual door for this book to be published. Your joy for life is infectious!

To Jim Rill, President of Milestones International Publishing—Thanks for your prayers and guidance and being willing to take a chance on publishing a girl whose main platform is the kitchen sink.

To Pastor Tommy and Marja Barnett—Thanks for loving my family like we have never been loved before! There are simply no adequate words to say how much you mean to us and how much we treasure the things you have taught us. Especially Jude 2.

To Pastor Leo and Molly—We have a healed marriage and a happy home, largely because of your ministry and prayers. We are forever grateful to you both and all the staff at NAME Ministries.

To Pastor Kristie Sexton—You are my treasure! Like a lifeline thrown at precisely the right moment, you have been to me. I am so blessed to know you. And to all the Phoenix Girl leadership and friends—It is an honor to serve together with passion in the house.

To Pastor Jeff and Rhonda Allaway—Thanks for the invitation to come to Adopt-a-Block. With that invitation you changed our lives! We are grateful to our entire Adopt-a-Block family.

To Pastor Jeff May and Jann—Thanks for being our Arizona family and for celebrating life together! Thanks for reminding us to dream again!

To Pastor Saeed and Cynthia Hosseini—For teaching us early to seek Him. You have provided a place where healing, restoration and dreams can be born!

To Jane Rucker—Thanks for all your hard work, diligence, and patience in the editing of this book and making this ten-year dream come true.

To my spiritual mothers and mentors: Kelli McCabe, Deloris Jordan, Mary Ann Hopkins, Nancy Hinkle, Margaret Lester, Faithe Tines, Anna Baker, and Lucy Knott—Thanks for being Titus 2 women to me and for your prayers, wisdom and guidance. And especially your time! You have poured unselfishly into my life.

To my family members and friends—You have loved and encouraged me in spite of myself. Thanks for putting up with me all these years!

To moms and spiritual moms who will read this book—I am grateful that you picked up *The Marvelous Madness of Motherhood*. I have prayed for you and believe it is no accident that you are reading this book. In the pages you will find my heart, but better still, I pray you find the heart of Christ. May you be blessed.

DEDICATION

To my mother, Bernice Davis

My husband, Edward

My children Davis, Hamilton, and Truett

And

Debi, Dena, and Jennifer—Keep on praying, girls!

TABLE OF CONTENTS

FOREWORD

Parenting often feels like a circus that involves juggling, balancing on tightropes, and taming lions, but it's a flying trapeze that I want to master and enjoy for the rest of my life. I remember a frantic day when my husband Bob and I rendezvoused at the coffee shop where one of our teenage sons worked. We were involved in a kid-exchange where I was picking up our two-year-old son. Bemoans to me, Bob was priming our little guy for a moment I wasn't necessarily prepared for. Frenzied, I ran into the populated coffee shop and was greeted by an extremely loud two-year-old voice clearly shouting, "You one hot mama!" Yeah, everyone checked me out–and it wasn't exactly impressive!

The pages you're about to experience will take you beyond trying to impress anyone and draw you into a journey of making the *most important impression of a lifetime*. Your moment-by-moment choices are molding your children–no matter what their age–and your investment will bring a return of rewards that are priceless and immeasurable.

I can't think of anyone more qualified to write this book than Becky Keener. She doesn't rely on qualified expertise to make her children picture perfect. She trusts God relentlessly, walks and talks with Him through her day, and lives a radically selfless life.

The proof is in the pudding! Her children are amazing, but she wrote this book for you. I know the desire of her heart is for you to feel loved, accepted, energized, and passionate about your high calling.

Life in the circus takes extreme talent, discipline, and a high level of skill–parenting on the other hand, involves a teachable heart, a desire to give, and an ability to keep peace through the storm. *Nobody* can parent alone; *everyone* has access to his or her ultimate parent, our Father in heaven. Embrace the journey, enjoy the moment, and remember to laugh!

Audrey and Bob Meisner
Authors of Bestseller, *Marriage Under Cover*

INTRODUCTION

A few years ago I asked a dear friend of mine—a pastor's wife and mother of five children, "Did your mom ever tell you how much work it was to be a mother?"

"No," she responded as our children all began whining and fighting around us at what seemed like the same time. "No, she did not."

"Neither did mine," I replied. "If women were to tell their daughters about what it *really* meant to be a mother and the work that is involved, our population just might decrease...rapidly!"

We laughed together because we knew that although motherhood can wring you out like a wet rag, it can also be incredibly rewarding. Children are without question a lavished gift of love from God (See Gen. 33:5). Some days the balancing act of being a mother, being a wife, working and having a life can be pretty maddening. But it can also be marvelous when we ask God to guide us and bring balance, order, and enjoyment.

In this book I share some spiritual and very practical tips on how to make the experience of motherhood an enjoyable one and how to train up your children in *the way* they should go (See Prov. 22:6). I have included some humorous insights to lighten the load and to bring reassurance to each mother that you are not alone in your quest to raise Godly children in the midst of an ungodly world and still manage to stay sane in the process.

Every mother needs to be reassured that God really does care about the mundane things of life that have to be done in order to care for a family. Motherhood truly is one of the highest callings on earth today and the saying may hold true that says, "the hand that rocks the cradle rules the world."

CHAPTER 1

THE MARVELOUS MADNESS OF BIRTHING CHILDREN

I will confess and praise You for You are fearful and wonderful and for the awful wonder of my birth! Wonderful are Your works, and that my inner self knows right well. My frame was not hidden from You when I was being formed in secret and intricately and curiously wrought (as if embroidered with various colors) in the depths of the earth (a region of darkness and mystery). Psalm 139:14-15 AMP

"The awful wonder of my birth." The psalmist sure got that right! Any mother who has birthed a child into the world can attest to the fact that birthing is an awful wonder. I have birthed three boys, and each experience was as unique as each child being born.

My oldest son, Davis, was born after twenty-five days in the hospital because my water broke at just thirty weeks of pregnancy. As a former marketing/public relations director for hospitals, it was a rare opportunity for me to see what it was like to experience the hospital as a patient.

We spent five days in a small rural hospital on total bed rest…complete with IVs, steroid injections and lots of contractions.

After five days of being in what they call "trindelinburg" position (flat on my back with my head lower than my feet), I was beginning to consider incorporating "trindelinburg" into my child's name. Even with all the doctors and nurses did to keep the baby from being born too soon, the contractions still persisted.

On Easter morning the doctor glumly announced (glum for me, happy for the staff!) that I would have to be transferred to another hospital in downtown Atlanta. So they put me into an ambulance, and away we went. The advice as we sped away was to try not to have the baby on the way…and to cross my legs!

Well, Davis didn't come on the way to the hospital, but rather, three weeks later. After days of false alarms, IVs, monitoring, amniocentesis, blood samples, bed pans, begging to get showers, longing to go outside, and lots of tears and laughter, I delivered Davis by C-section early on the morning of April 22.

He was immediately incubated and taken to the neo-natal nursery where he promptly spit out the respirator, announcing to everyone that he was healthy and strong and would not tolerate all that hoopla. He was feisty from the start, but is without question one of the most spiritually sensitive and sweet boys you would ever want to meet. We say he's our John, the Beloved. He has a special call on his life and has announced quite frequently that he is going to be like Billy Graham one day. Maybe that's why the enemy seemed to fight his birth so much.

There were lots of very low and lonely days in that hospital two hours away from family and friends, but God was there. He was right there with me in that hospital room every day to comfort me and brighten my day. He brought Holy Spirit-filled nurses to care for me and to pray over me when the contractions would start coming.

One of my nurses was an incredible woman of God from Nigeria. For fun and to help pass the time, I made up a little song using the tune to "Old MacDonald Had a Farm" with her name. When she would come into the room I would sing it out really loud, and she'd sing back, "E-I-E-I-O!" Then we'd laugh and laugh.

See, God gave me this wonderful woman as a gift, a Holy Spirit-filled nurse who would say in her African dialect, "In the name of Jesus" over me when I was having a difficult day. God made provision to get me through a very scary time in my life. He was there in her.

He was also there in my husband who would dress up and hide in the hospital closet and jump out to kid with the nurses to get a laugh. God was definitely there in my husband when he brought Oreo Cheesecake!

And God was there in my precious mother who would come and stay with me and endure my bad moods and being awakened by the nurses several times a night. God was in my mother the day I announced that I was getting a shower despite the doctor's orders not to get out of bed. I asked my little mother who had never done a disobedient thing in her life, to hold the door to the outside so the doctor and the nurses couldn't catch me sneaking into the bathroom.

Carrying my IV unit with me and holding my gown closed in the back, I made it to the bathroom. As soon as I was in there, what do you know? A surprise visit from my doctor! He pushed the door open despite my mother's resistance and stepped inside the room. Realizing I was not in my bed, the doctor yelled loudly, "Where is the patient?"

My mother, frightened to death, almost shrieked, "I don't know!"

Then pointing to the bathroom door, the doctor yelled back as if he had caught a thief, "She's in there!"

By that time, I had forgotten that I was a Christian and was over the edge. Twenty some days in the hospital being poked with needles, using bed pans, lying trapped in the "trindelinberg" position had taken a toll. I came out of that bathroom with my IV pole, holding the back of my gown and announced with an expletive or two, "Yes, I am in the bathroom, and there's nothing you can do about it!" Realizing that he was dealing with a mad pregnant woman, the doctor backed down.

And God was right there the day Davis was born and touched his little five-pound body and his lungs with super miracle strength so he would only have to spend hours in the ICU instead of the predicted days. His birth was an *awful wonder* and he is a blessing and miracle to us.

My second baby, Hamilton Monroe Keener, came out a toddler and walking! Born normal delivery after ten hours of labor, he weighed eight pounds, four ounces. He seemed so very strong to me compared to our first baby. I delivered at the same hospital where I was originally cared for with the first pregnancy. I even had the same doctor. He was rather glad and hopeful that I would be able to have a normal delivery and wanted to make the experience as good as possible.

Being golf buddies, my husband and my physician did a little joking around as we were waiting for the baby to come. This didn't seem to ease the labor for me, but it seemed to do wonders for them. I have a picture of the two of them holding up a dilation chart where they had drawn a smiley face on number ten. I could tell that this birth would be an awesome wonder.

At one point during the labor my blood pressure and heart rate, as well as the baby's, fell dangerously low. The nurses made me get on my hands and knees (a lovely thought!). My mother and a friend in the room began to pray. When the situation didn't improve, the nurse turned and yelled, "Keep praying!" Almost as quickly as my heart rate had dropped, it began to rise. God did answer our prayers that day, and Hamilton was born not long after, very healthy and strong.

He has the most incredible red hair and gorgeous brown eyes. It seems since the day he could walk until now, Hamilton is found dressed up as a super hero or Bible Man with a sword in his hand. He has the biggest, most thoughtful, loving heart and the loudest mouth you could imagine.

Because he is the middle child, we've made a big deal about him being special because he not only has an older sibling, but a younger one, too—something the other two cannot claim. With so many people talking about the middle child syndrome, we make a point of telling him that he is our "Double Stuff"—you know, like the middle of an Oreo! Some would argue that this is the best part....

He has lots of other nicknames like Hammy, Bubba, and Bones, but when I think of who in the Bible he might be like, I think of a warrior, Gideon. Gideon was fierce and strong like Hamilton, who oddly displays a great interest in watching the military channel on TV. And his birth was an *awful wonder.*

My third and last baby, Jonathan Truett, was born four years later in Phoenix, Arizona. Away from the familiar small town hospital, doctors, family and friends, I thought *Well, I will have to have this baby on my own.* It was just my husband and me in a big hospital where no one knew us and I didn't know them.

When the contractions started coming, I remember having that "I want my mama" feeling, but she was thousands of miles away back in Georgia. Although I knew my parents and others were praying for me, I sensed that this would be something I would have to go through on my own with the Holy Spirit. Edward and I were going through an incredible crisis in our marriage and finances at that time and my whole world had been turned upside down. I felt I had no one but God.

When the anesthesiologist came in to give me the epidural, I was rather relieved. As he put the "ten-foot-long" needle in my back, Edward was standing at the bedside holding my hand. All of a sudden, I saw him begin turning white and I felt his hand in mine go limp. I was trying to hold him up with my arm to keep him from fainting and falling on the floor. The needle was in my back and the anesthesiologist was yelling, "Don't move!" So, with a choice between "paralyzation" or letting my husband fall on the floor, I chose to do what any good wife in labor would do—I let him hit the floor!

Several hours later Jonathan Truett was born eight pounds, fifteen ounces—the biggest baby yet. He was beautiful and the nurses made a great to do over him and asked if they could hold him at the nurses station. Exhausted, I said, "Yes. Please! Take him!"

Jonathan Truett as we call him, named after a great man of God and an entrepenuar, Truett Cathy, has been a great joy to our family. I called him Jonathan because, like Jonathan in the Bible, he is a covenant baby. He has been a "place" where my husband and I could go together in a storm with no hurt, disagreement or strife. I believe he was sent from heaven like an arrow at a strategic time. His birth brought healing and hope to our family and was an *awful wonder.*

One thing is for sure, children are a wonderful work of God and they were formed by His hand in secret. The Scripture goes on to say, *Wonderful are Your works, and that my inner self knows right well.* (Psalm 139:14 AMP) The birth of a child is an *awful wonder* and sometimes it is good to recount the miracle of it all. Were you to ask one hundred women to tell their experience in birthing, you would get a hundred different answers. Each experience is unique to you. That's how God intended it to be.

Take some time to record the awesome wonder of your birth and, if you are a mother, the birth of your child or children.

Pray and ask God to help you treasure your children and to see them as the wonder that they truly are!

A Mother's Prayer

Father God, as You have shown us in Psalm 139, You have knit our children together perfectly. You made them in secret and have given them to us as a gift to value and to treasure. You have wondrously brought our children into our lives. We give You praise for our children and for the awesomeness of their birth.

We speak a blessing over them to live a life rich with Your presence. We bless them to health and prosperity, happiness, honor and favor all the days of their lives.

Help us to raise them in Your admonition and to dedicate ourselves and our babies and our grandbabies back to You. We pray that our lives may be used for Your service and Your glory always.

In Jesus' name we pray. Amen.

CHAPTER 2

THE MARVELOUS MADNESS OF BABY DAZE

Lo, children are an heritage of the Lord; and the fruit of the womb is his reward. Psalm 127:3

I reminded myself of that Scripture A LOT when my children were babies! Through every season of their babyhood there seemed to be a new challenge and experience waiting around the bend. They are truly a heritage from the Lord and angels sent from heaven, but the sleepless weeks that follow make you feel at moments that they are straight from somewhere else. You find yourself in a fog of sorts, something I call the *baby daze*.

It begins shortly after the euphoria of the delivery and sometimes lasts for the entire first year of the baby's life. Some more fortunate moms seem to shake the baby daze around the sixth month. When my third child was nearly two years old, I still had a bad case of the baby daze. My forty-year-old body just didn't seem to bounce back and keep up with the demands of three active boys and a husband like I used to.

Not many mothers tell their daughters the real details about the delivery or the months that follow. It is my theory that by the time a mother gets to be a grandmother, she has completely blocked out the painful or tiring memories of the birthing and rearing of children and chooses only to remember the delight.

Baby daze comes from the 2:00 AM and 4:00 AM diaper changes and feedings and the feeling that you are the only one on the face of the earth awake at that moment. It comes from hormonal changes that just seem to "bottom out" about the fifth or sixth week after having the baby. It comes from walking into the laundry room and feeling like you could pass out from the piles around you. It comes from the aches and pains and shifts of your bones trying to return to their original state (which they never do). It especially hits after the excitement of a new baby wanes and the grandparents all go home. It comes from that overwhelming feeling of *How am I ever going to care for all these children myself?*

Lack of sleep overwhelmed me with our first baby after being in the hospital a month. Nurses would come in all through the night to wake the baby or me for tests. One of the night nurses with whom I had become especially fond, came in around two in the morning to see the baby. Affected so badly at this point by baby daze—and half out of my mind from all the needles and tests—I, in a sleepy fog, yelled at her at the top of my lungs, "Hey, what are you doing in here? Get out of here. Don't touch my baby!" I didn't know at the moment that she had brought a pair of booties she had lovingly knitted for the baby.

Edward, slightly more awake than I, said, "Becky, the nurse has just come in to see the baby. She's leaving and it's her last chance to say goodbye to us. Calm down." When I finally woke up and realized what I had done, I was so embarrassed, especially as she handed me the beautifully wrapped box with the hand-knitted booties inside.

I felt like a worm! I still feel embarrassed to this day! I blame it on baby daze. My husband said, "Reckon (that's southern for *do you think*) **she** (the nurse) ever got over it?"

This baby daze syndrome hit me hard with our third baby. My oldest son caught a bad case of the flu just as I was in the hospital delivering. Needless to say, when the baby and I came home from the hospital, I had my hands full. I put the "sick patient" downstairs, throwing up and running a high fever. The new baby came upstairs with me. My husband had no choice but to return to work, and there were no grandparents around at that time to help out.

One day out of the hospital and I was up and down the steps crying like a baby, asking God, "Where are You?" It all seems so traumatic at the time, yet looking back on it now, it's kind of funny. Sometimes we get in such a self-pity funk and can't even enjoy the blessing and the wonder of new life in our home.

At my six-week checkup, my doctor took one look at me and said, "You are depressed! It's postpartum depression." He recommended either I attend a support group or go on an anti-depressant.

Being too depressed to talk about it at a support group, I chose the anti-depressant. After just one dose, I decided that the anti-depressant wasn't for me either. It seemed that I was moving in slow motion, but my children were all moving at warp speed. It was scary.

I believe it is important for a new mom to know that you are going to experience the gamut of emotions after the delivery of your baby. Some of those emotions range from elation to deflation! I'm just going to tell you straight up because nobody else will want to break it to you. The combination of sleepless nights, hormonal changes in your body, care of other children, and other life changes such as finances or stressful relationships can wear you down.

The very best thing you can do for yourself is to SLOW DOWN. Don't try to maintain normal activity the first three months after a baby is born. Don't place unreasonable expectations on yourself or others. Don't expect your home to be a picture of perfection. Don't expect the meals to be cooked every day as normal. Simplify your life to spend more quiet time. Sleep when the baby sleeps if possible. If you have other small children, make them nap, too! They need the rest and, especially you do, too. Spend more time in the Word of God. You need mega doses at this time. By that I mean numerous chapters a day. Spend time just sitting in God's presence holding the baby. Turn on praise music and just sit or lie down and let your body heal. Your body needs that time to get back to normal.

This is not the time to return to work immediately after the baby, to entertain, to go a lot of places dragging a new baby around. This is a time to be quiet and let your body rest and heal. I hear so many stories from friends who, like me, felt they had to have a perfect home, entertain a stream of visitors after the baby, and return every phone call—or worse yet, return to work. About the fifth week of trying to keep this up, the weary mother usually crashes emotionally and physically.

A newborn baby in the home is such a blessing in so many ways. It seems that everything just slows down when a new baby arrives. The time that they are babies is so fleeting, if we don't slow down we miss it. Someone gave me a beautiful wall hanging at the birth of my third son. It reads: *A new baby is God's opinion the world should go on.* Babies reaffirm the wonder and the power of Almighty God and that no one but Him could ever accomplish such a feat as to create that perfection we see in new life. Even the smell of a new baby is angelic and somewhat unearthly, as if the child had just come from the presence of God Himself. And I am convinced that they do! When my third son was a small baby, we were certain that he was able to see the presence of angels. When he turned two years old, he often would comment, "I see the angels!"

As a mother of young children, I tried to remind myself of the Scriptures Jesus spoke in regard to babes and children. In Mark 10:14 He said, *Let the little children come unto me.* What He was saying there was, "Children are a delight to Me; I enjoy them and I want them around My ministry." He was saying, "They need to be close to Me and I need to be close to them." I believe Jesus enjoyed their playfulness, their innocence, their laughter, and even their cries and whines. Contrary to much of our society today, Jesus valued children and their presence. I believe He viewed them as an essential element of His ministry while on earth.

Psalm 127:3 says that children are a heritage, which means an heirloom or portion. Our portion means we are to take it all in and enjoy it. The Psalm goes on to say that children are the fruit of our womb. The word *fruit* implies that some work has been done and now we are to enjoy the harvest. That's why they call the birthing process *labor*. It is work. When the work has been done, it is time to enjoy the *harvest* or the *fruit*.

Slow down and enjoy your new baby. Enjoy watching your other children if you have them, enjoying the new baby. Allow your body to heal and you will not miss God's great gift of a new baby in your home.

List at least three ways that you can slow down and enjoy your children. You may have to cut out some activities for a season, but consider some ways that you can get more balance in your life, especially if you have a new baby or toddler in the house.

____

____

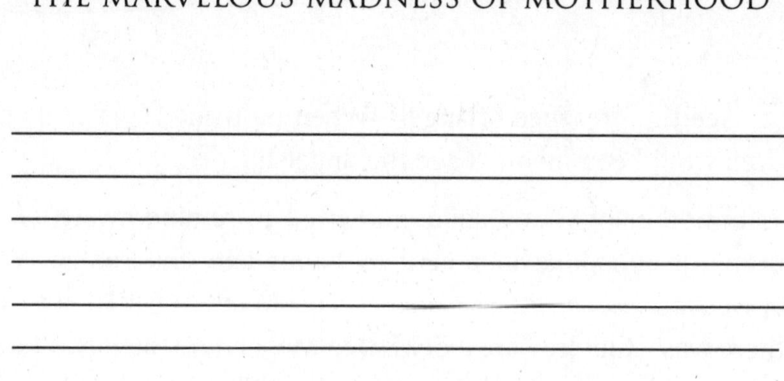

A Mother's Prayer

Father God, help me to slow down and recognize that the time my children are small is only brief. Help me to enjoy them to the fullest measure and to rest in You. Thank You for giving me the rest and the sleep that I need to be a patient, kind, and alert parent. Help me to delight in their playfulness, their innocence and their laughter. And thank You for helping me to remain calm in their crying and moments of frustration.

I speak a blessing over them that they will be peaceful and calm throughout the days of their lives. I thank You, God, for molding me and making me into the mother that You would have me to be.

In Jesus' name I pray. Amen.

CHAPTER 3

THE MARVELOUS MADNESS OF THE SOUNDS OF CHILDREN

From the lips of babes you have perfected praise. Mat. 21:16b

With three small boys in the house, there seems to always be a lot of noise! Either they are all chasing each other through the house with swords, or they are wrestling, or throwing footballs, or jumping on beds (or worse, the furniture), or fighting one another and screaming at the top of their lungs. After a few years of motherhood, I am beginning to get it through my head that children are noisy and that's the way it is going to be for a while.

My mother never warned me about how noisy it was going to be with three children and all their friends in the house. Maybe that's because after raising three children of her own, she never really seemed to notice that much. If she did, she never seemed to let on to us. She never yelled, "Shut up!" at the top of her lungs, as I have. Most of the time she just "happily" said "Go outside and play." My mother really was a picture of Jesus in my life. She just seemed to remain stable in her emotions and not "freak out" as so many of my friends and I have admitted to doing. After the birth of my second son, she did gently say to me that there were going to have to be a few things I learn to ignore. (Wonder where she could have come up with that notion!)

I remember as a little girl going to my Grandmother Helen's farm in South Georgia. We would usually go for the summer, holidays and frequent weekends to meet my mom's sister, Aunt Madeline. (I call her Aunt Sukey.) There were seven grandchildren in all who invaded my grandparents' home, and we were usually there together. We'd spend a large portion of our summer there working in the garden and canning. The grandchildren would play together and chase each other up and down the wood-floored hallways of the old farmhouse. We would play hide-and-seek in and out of the house and LOUDLY scream and laugh and enjoy being together with family. Grandfather would let us all ride in the back of his truck to feed the cows. Along the way we'd sing at the top of our lungs, usually led by Aunt Sukey (a school teacher for more than thirty-five years). Some of my happiest childhood memories are those I have of being at my grandmother's farm where we children felt so free to laugh and love and sing. And we usually had one volume—very loud!

In the words *From the lips of babes you have perfected praise*, Jesus was saying so much. There are layers of meaning in what He was saying here to the Pharisees. He was saying that you did not have to be mature—either in spiritual or in physical terms—in order to offer perfect praise. The word Jesus used here for *perfected* actually means *to complete thoroughly* or *to restore.* In each new life, there is that possibility of a new life restored back to God. The Greek meaning for the word *babes* in this incidence meant either *small children* or *those who were new believers in Christ*.

The use of the word *lips* in the Scripture is very interesting. The function of lips is to form words and speak either blessing or cursing, life or death. Jesus could have said that from the heart of babes or from the mind of babes, from the physical bodies of babes, or from the life of babes—but He chose to say *from the lips.* The part of the body which forms the very words used to confess life and belief in Jesus as our Lord and Saviour is the lips. This very small part of the body can also get us into the most trouble through cursing, gossip, negative words and confessions. God created the entire universe by speaking it into existence. The circumstances of our life can be changed by our lips!

Recently my mother and I were discussing the story of Hannah, the mother of Samuel in the Bible. In the first chapter of First Samuel, we see Hannah longing so deeply for a child that she bares her heart utterly to God, speaking to Him her vow of dedication, speaking so deeply from within her heart that her lips moved without sound. She already had a mother's heart, a mother's heart commitment toward her child. These words she spoke to God in her heart, even though they were without sound, affected all of Samuel's life.

The loud voices of children can be excruciatingly painful at times. It seems that they have built-in microphones on their mouths. Their cries, their whines, their screams, their sassing, their fighting—all can drive a mother completely over the edge at times. Numerous times a day, you can hear me saying, "Hush your mouth!" And if I've really had it, I might say, "Shut up!" which is the equivalent to a cuss word in our home! With my three boys, there is usually only one volume—very, very loud. There is always noise from the moving of their lips and most of the time it doesn't sound like praise. In sheer exasperation, my mother-in-law used to say to my husband when he was a little boy, "If you don't hush, I am going to mash your mouth all over your face." (That's pretty funny when you get the visual.)

Part of the calling of motherhood is to hear the perfected praise on the lips of our children. Even when we are so tired of hearing their "little" voices, to know that Jesus loves and values the fruit of their lips. The point Jesus was making to the Pharisees in this passage is that each life is important and valuable in the sight of God and that each baby brings a perfection of praise to His ears.

Jesus taught us the value of a life whether blind, lame, sinful, or religiously stubborn as the Pharisees were. Babies are not knowledgeable about Scripture or religious rituals. Children just simply trust and laugh, with innocent belief and humility that their needs will be met. That's why Jesus said that unless you are a saved little child, you cannot enter heaven (See Matthew 18:3).

When a baby is born, we are totally dependent on the caregiver for food, warmth, medical care, and affection. Babies seem to have an innate understanding of who God is that wanes as they get older if their spirit man is not nurtured with the Word of God. Jesus is saying to us as adults to get back to that carefree trust, knowing that He is in control and will meet all our needs.

It is so important for us daily to pray for our children, to speak and teach the Word of God to them, to speak a blessing over them every day. Our job is to help restore, repair and rekindle their love and relationship with God that can so easily be taken out of them. We are to lead them to a personal relationship with Jesus Christ. This is our highest calling as a Christian mother. We must always point our children back to God, in every circumstance and situation, taking every opportunity to teach them about God and His plan for their lives.

Secondly, we must teach our children that Jesus said that from the fruit of their lips He has perfected praise. Their praise is important to God and He desires to hear them praising. Teach your children, even as babies, to raise their hands and participate in praising in your home, your car, your worship services. Their lives will be forever changed when they connect to God through praise.

Lastly, as a mother of young children, I would encourage you to listen for the praise in your child's voice and laughter. Even when nerves are frayed, we can stop and remind ourselves that *from the lips of babes he has ordained praise* (Psalm 8:2 NIV).

Sometimes you may have a child who seems to be whinier or crankier than another child and it becomes necessary to train that child to be joyful. Our third son, Truett, had a difficult time with this when he was very small. At times it felt like if he was awake, he was crying. When he learned how to talk, he would say, "Mama, I cwied and I cwied and I cwied," all the while moving his hands in a circular motion very dramatically. We would say back to him, "Oh, don't cry. You laughed and you laughed and you laughed." We literally had to retrain him to stop all the whining and the crying and to be a joyful baby.

On a recent busy morning before school, I was rushing around getting breakfast, packing lunches and getting backpacks ready, finding socks...you know how it is. Meanwhile my children were chasing each other and laughing hysterically. At first I felt somewhat frustrated that they were having such a grand ole time while I was working so hard to get them ready for school. Then all of a sudden, the Holy Spirit brought this Scripture to my remembrance. As they were laughing I heard Him say, "Their laughter is the sound of praise and the sound of your success as a mother."

That word of encouragement to my heart from the Holy Spirit reminded me of the fact that from their lips is praise perfected, and it has changed my outlook on noise in my home. Mother, when it's appropriate, free your children from bondages as Jesus was doing the day He confronted the Pharisees. Let them laugh and play. Free them to love life and to praise God with everything that is within them. It changes an atmosphere and it changes lives.

I close this chapter with my youngest singing at the top of his lungs *My Redeemer lives! My Lord has conquered the grave!* This has gone on for the last ten minutes until his voice is nearly hoarse and my husband asked him to quiet it down a little. Wow! He's really changed the atmosphere around here. Suddenly, I realize we've come a long way from *I cwied and I cwied*!

When are the times that the noise from your children becomes a source of irritation?

____

____

____

____

Write one way you can change your perception of their noise from irritation to praise.

____

____

____

____

Note some practical ways you can teach your children to actively participate in praise and worship.

____

____

____

____

A Mother's Prayer

Father God, I thank You for making our home a peaceful place and a place of praise. Help me to hear Your voice and Your laughter amid the laughter and noise of my children.

I speak a blessing over my children that they will use their voices to bring praise and not discord. I bless them that they be children of praise, joy, and laughter all their days.

Thank You for helping me to recognize that from the lips of babes You have ordained praise. Help me to enjoy this noise to the fullest, even when it doesn't harmonize, recognizing that in a few short years, the noise will have grown up and moved away. Thank You for the treasure of their voices in my home.

In Jesus' name I pray. Amen

CHAPTER 4

THE MARVELOUS MADNESS OF HOUSEKEEPING WITH CHILDREN

"Who put the football in the refrigerator?"

"Who wrote on the dining room chairs with permanent marker?"

"Who left the dirty socks on the breakfast table?"

"Who squeezed toothpaste all over the sink?"

"Who pee-peed on the bathroom wall?"

"Who threw rocks in the pool?"

"Who put the gum on the carpet?"

"Who rubbed Jell-O on the coffee table?"

"Who got into Dad's shaving cream?"

"Who used a whole bottle of shampoo?"

"Who poured soda all over the back seat of the van?"

"Who put the sucker in my bed?"

"Who blew their nose and threw down the tissue?"

"Who put peanut butter in the DVD player?"

"Who threw spaghetti noodles all over the kitchen floor?"

"Who took all the books off the shelf?"

"Whose wet towel is this on the floor?"

"Who put the string cheese wrappers in the sofa cushions?"

"Who dropped Cheetos all over the carpet in the living room?"

"Who threw the 'gack splat' on the ceiling?"

"Why are there five drink glasses on your night stand?"

"Why did you leave your backpack and shoes in the middle of the floor?"

"Who stuck a pencil in the side of their soda cup (with the drink still inside)?"

"Who put pennies in the fax machine?"

"Who left Dad's tools all over the yard?"

"Who wrote on my computer screen?"

"Who put the Legos in the oven?"

These are but a few of the questions in my life as a mother. If you are a mother, you have your own list, too!

Sometimes I feel that I am a bit outnumbered in my home. There are three little people who are not concerned about how our home looks and one (that would be me) who is frantically trying to go behind them and salvage my hopes and dreams for living in a neat, beautiful home. Since I was a little girl, I have scanned the pages of *Southern Living*, admiring the meticulously decorated houses, trying to achieve what was on those pages. Now, three children later, I am realizing that my *expectations* of living everyday life in a magazine picture is just not realistic.

Even with lowered expectations, I continue to be blown away by the amount of destruction a child can do to a home. I am amazed at how quickly my house can return to a messy unkempt state after I've spent hours doing housecleaning. There are days when the business of keeping a clean home seems quite futile. I have allowed myself to get very emotional about it all, which seems to further desensitize my children's desire to care about the house. I have even tried going on strike, saying that if they don't care about our home, then neither will I; I'll just let it go. That doesn't work either because I cannot think, let alone thrive, in a mess. And it seems that the days I decide to go on strike are the very days when a friend or a neighbor will drop by. They are aghast at the state of my home and I am completely humiliated.

Sometimes I am amazed that this is my life right now with young children. I never pictured motherhood or my life being quite like this. The constant work will make even the strongest among us weak-kneed. I laughingly tell my girlfriends that it would take a *team* of women several days to *really* clean my home. I spend most of my cleaning time picking up clothes, shoes, toys, towels, school papers, backpacks, trash, and food. It could take a good three hours just to make beds and pick up the house, let alone actually clean!

The other day I was on my hands and knees under the breakfast table scraping dried Cheerios off the carpet. I was reminded of a scene from one of my favorite movies, a comedy called *Overboard* with Goldie Hawn and Kurt Russell. In the movie Goldie, who plays a very rich woman with no children, falls off her yacht and is taken to the hospital with amnesia. Kurt Russell's character, who is angry with her because she failed to pay him for work done on her yacht, decides to bring her home in revenge to "slave" for him and his four boys in his run-down home. He tries to convince her that she is really his wife and the mother of the boys.

He goes over a list of daily chores that she is responsible for to help her relearn her daily routine. The first day in her new home she cooked and cleaned and scrubbed a home that hadn't been cared for at all by the five "men." After several days of this routine, Goldie's character finally has a breakdown of sorts and is unable to speak from the "torture." After he dunks her in an outdoor water barrel to regain consciousness, she comes up saying, "I can't DO these vile things, and even if I could, I wouldn't want to!"

How many moms can identify with that feeling! "I can't do these vile things!" I made the mistake of saying that in front of my eight-year-old recently and he retorted rather quickly, "But Mom, you can do all things through Christ who strengthens you."

I don't think any young bride, hoping to become a mom, has any thought about the responsibility or the amount of work it takes to set up and maintain a home or to care for children. It's work, baby! It's back-breaking, sweat-breaking, and sometimes heartbreaking. But, oh how rewarding it can be! I have worked in quite a number of different jobs before and I can tell you (young brides, new moms, and hoping-to-be mothers) that the work of motherhood is, without a doubt, the most fulfilling of them all.

It's fulfilling for many reasons, but probably the greatest fulfillment for me is found in the Scripture, *Train up a child in the way he should go, and when he is old he will not depart from it* (Prov. 22:6). I believe this means primarily to train up a child in the Word of God, but I like to apply it to the practical things of life as well.

Training is different from teaching in that, when you teach someone, you give them information through lectures, classes, or some other form of communication. But when you *train* someone in how to do something, a skill is passed on to them by demonstrating to them how to do it, by doing it with them until they get the idea, and then by stepping back and observing them as they do it—even if they don't do it perfectly the first, second, third or even fourth time.

Training is one answer to every mother's housekeeping prayers. A maid service would be the second! However, that's not always financially feasible. Training your child to help take care of your home is the key to bringing order out of chaos and fostering respect for the things God has given us. It is the key to having that home we have always hoped of having, one that is clean, comfortable and warm. When you train a child to do a particular chore or task, you are equipping them with life skills which will bless them forever. Many times, it is so much easier to do the job yourself and gripe about it than it is to *train* a child in the way he/she should go. But children are so capable of helping to keep a neat orderly home and they need to learn the skills for proper development.

When my oldest son was in the second grade, his very Godly teacher noticed some areas in which he was struggling. She suggested that we assign him a "really big task" with a title that would cause him to rise to the occasion. We decided to make him the "Head of Recycling" in our home. This assignment helped give Davis a sense of confidence and self-esteem as well as developing much needed leadership skills.

My four-year-old (at that time) became the "Chief Table Setter." We have stayed with these job assignments, and of course, added more as they have grown. Even our two-year-old is capable of watering plants, taking laundry to the laundry room, picking up toys, wiping up messes, and straightening a room. All with just a little training.

One of the things I have learned in getting my children's help without getting the whining, too, is to temper it with positive encouragement. I may say something like, "Truett, thanks for being such a great helper to Mommy! Do you think you could help me again and take your toys to your room?" Let me tell you, girls, it works *almost* every time! Those five little words—"Can you be Mommy's helper?"—make all the difference in the world with younger children. Try it!

One of my friends and mentors once said to me, "Don't be afraid to make your children work. It will do them good." Training a child to assist with the everyday tasks of life like folding laundry, sweeping the driveway, pulling weeds, making beds, loading a dishwasher, dusting or cleaning helps them to feel a sense of ownership about their life and their home. And it encourages them to be a team player.

In a world where entertaining kids has become a billion dollar business with theme parks, video games, movies and so much more, training our kids to work and to be responsible adults can become passé. We're afraid that we'll warp them if they have to work too much or damage their self-esteem. Just the opposite is true. We'd do well to teach our children Proverbs 14:23 which tells us that those who work hard make a profit, but those who only talk (or in my house, watch too much TV) will be poor. You wind up with spoiled children and a tired cranky parent who is laboring to do the work of a household by himself/herself.

If that's you, stop robbing your children of the chance to learn. Train them up in the way they should go, and when they are old, they will not depart from it. Train them to do specific chores each day and to respect your home and furnishings. It will make life much happier for the entire family.

As for rewards or allowance, you have to set up what works best for you and your family. When faced with a serious financial crisis, my husband and I were not able to pay a weekly allowance to our children. We began encouraging them with small rewards and by telling them that as members of our family, they were expected to participate in taking care of our home. This has seemed to work best for us rather than the weekly allowance, especially since they were always looking for a "raise."

While I myself need great improvement in this area of allowances and money management, I will say that giving allowances is important for us all to learn the value of a dollar. A great idea I heard from a Christian financial advisor was to give your children their allowance in dollar bills. Then put three containers for each child in their rooms. Label one with "Tithe," one with "Save," and one with "Spend." Have the child learn to first put ten percent of their allowance into the "Tithe" container and ten percent into the "Save" container. This teaches a lifelong skill that I would have been better off learning from the time I was a child. This is part of training up a child.

As I close this chapter, I am compelled to go and practice even more what I have preached on training up a child. My two-year-old has broken my thoughts numerous times. I have stopped to break up a fight between him and our middle child. I've popped popcorn for their movie and swept up a treasured wedding gift which was broken on the tile. I mopped up after the "baby" took off his diaper and pee-peed on the floor. Whew! I'm exhausted! Sounds like some serious training is in order!

Just for fun, record a few of your own "Who put this…?" and "Who did that…?" questions, as I have at the beginning of the chapter.

____

____

____

Name the children in your home and their ages and list some specific age-appropriate tasks for them to do. Also write a reward that you would like to give at the end of the week, i.e., allowance, ice cream, movie, etc.

Write the homemaking skills you would like to train your children to do and at what age.

A Mother's Prayer

Father God, I thank You for a roof over our heads, for a place to call home. And I thank You for the privilege of keeping it clean and orderly for You. Thank You for the wisdom and understanding to know how to train my children in the way they should go.

I speak a blessing over my children that they would enjoy a clean comfortable home—a place of beauty and order of their own one day. I speak a blessing over them that they will be diligent and hard workers all their days.

Thank You for for helping me train them how to desire and to have a clean, orderly, Godly home, making sure that all we do brings glory and honor to You. Thank You for giving me the skills I need to run our home with happy efficiency so that we as a family are ready in season and out of season to extend Your love and hospitality to others.

In Jesus' name I pray. Amen.

CHAPTER 5

THE MARVELOUS MADNESS OF LAUNDRY AND CHILDREN

They that wait on the Lord,... they will walk and not faint. Isaiah 40:31

I have often thought I should post this Scripture above the door of my laundry room in plain view, "They will walk and not faint." On any given day during the week, I can find at least a load or two waiting to be washed, another load to be ironed, and another pile to be mended or donated. As I look at the piles, a feeling known in the South as "swimmy headed" seems to come over me. In other words, I feel like I could faint.

There are towels, sheets, dish towels, dust towels, delicates, dozens of jeans, shorts, tee shirts, my husband's work shirts, and bright colors all separated into their appropriate piles. Sometimes in frustration, I just cram them all in together, say a prayer, and hope it all turns out all right. Many of my husband's dress shirts have turned up mysteriously missing after being ruined in one of those combined wash specials.

Keeping up with the laundry for a family is an overwhelming task. Sometimes I cry out when I see all those piles. Sometimes I close the door and pretend I didn't see them. I get weary with my children and the many times they can change clothes during a day. They toss the "old" outfit, worn merely hours, onto a pile in the laundry room. There's usually, at some point, an old wet towel thrown on top of it so that, even though the worn clothes were still clean, they now must be washed. It almost feels like a conspiracy!

Adding to the challenge of laundry is the fact that, in order to conserve energy and save on my electric bill, I must do the laundry between the hours of 9:00 PM and 9:00 AM during weekdays or on weekends. Usually the last load in the dryer at night is unloaded and left on a chair to cool and to be folded full of wrinkles in the morning. *So what,* I usually say to myself as I hurriedly fold the wrinkled load. *I have boys and they couldn't care less if their clothes are wrinkled or not.*

Part of my laundry dilemma stems from the fact that I have too many clothes! Most of us have too many clothes! There are lots of clothes we don't wear because they don't fit or are completely out of style, but then there are those items that we continue to wear, but that look totally wrong on us. We wind up washing loads and piles that we really shouldn't even have been wearing. I caught myself grumbling to a friend not long ago, "I have a lot of fashionable clothes in my closet. Problem is, they were in fashion ten years ago!"

Recently I was reading some of Paul's writings in the New Testament. He said in 2 Corinthians 11:27 that he had been through shipwrecks, imprisonment, hunger and nakedness. Just for a moment I began to ponder what dear beloved Paul would think if he himself were able to physically walk into my closet today. I imagine he would be astonished by the clothes, shoes and accessories. We are so blessed and so rich, and don't even recognize it.

Here are three tips I try to abide by when it comes to laundry. They might be helpful to you in keeping your laundry under control and to help you keep from fainting when you step into your laundry room!

1. Wash a load and fold a load every day.

When you wash a load, you are putting one in the washer and usually taking one load out of the washer to be put into the dryer. To put a load in the dryer, you must take a load out and fold it. By using this rule daily, you are actually handling three loads each day. If you have a household of four or more, usually it will take this amount of attention to the laundry in order for it to stay under control and not get out of hand.

2. Give away everything you do not wear or need.

You know that old rationale of *it will come back in style someday* doesn't always work. The same with the one that says *I'll lose weight and it will fit.* Hey, listen to me; give those clothes away. After working with the homeless and poor for the past few years in my church's Adopt-a-Block program, I can tell you that the need is profound. If we only realized that something hanging in our closet not being worn can bless someone else so much, we would not hang onto it. Our women's ministry at church began cleaning out our closets and giving away nice complete outfits that other women could wear. Our efforts resulted in racks and racks of clothes, shoes, purses, and accessories for other women and moms to enjoy! We brought them all together on our church buses for a special Mother's Day luncheon and gave them shopping bags to shop to their heart's content! The pleasure and satisfaction of watching these moms shop far exceeds any shopping trip I have ever been blessed with myself! Maybe you might want to do something like this in your church.

3. Limit your children to one outfit a day.

Trying to enforce this rule is easier said than done. My middle child, Hamilton, has been known to change clothes four and five times a day. He is my "dress-up-king"! By limiting the number of clothing items they wear each day, you reduce your wash load. Children can learn to refold and hang clothes that have been worn slightly in a day, but don't need to be washed.

What are some changes you would like to make in regard to caring for and keeping the task of laundry under control?

____
____
____
____
____
____
____

What convictions, if any, do you feel about maintaining more order and balance in the purchase and care of your family's wardrobe?

____
____
____
____
____

A Mother's Prayer

Father God, help me to remember Your promise in Isaiah 40:31 that I will walk and not faint. Help me to remember this as I walk into my laundry room late at night to tackle a few loads after everyone has already gone to bed. Help me, God, to be thankful that we are blessed with clothes to maintain. Thank You for never failing to provide the clothes we need, when we need them.

Help us, God, to not worry about our wardrobe or fuss over what we wear, making fashion an idol. Help us to dress in such a way that it will always bring praise, glory and honor to You. Help me as a mother to train my children to appreciate the clothing You provide and to be good stewards over what You give us.

I speak a blessing over my children that all their needs will be met as You have promised to provide for us. I thank You that we, as a family, will be able to bless others in need and to be Christ's hands extended in this earth.

In Jesus' name I pray. Amen.

CHAPTER 6

THE MARVELOUS MADNESS OF TRAVELING WITH CHILDREN

Making request, if by any means now at length I might have a prosperous journey by the will of God to come unto you. For I long to see you, that I may impart unto you some spiritual gift, to the end ye may be established. Romans 1:10-11

I was remembering some of the wonderful trips God has blessed us with through the years and the ability to take our children with us. Some of the trips have been contests that my husband won through work and others were vacations we took as family or with friends. As a family, we've been on cruises to the Bahamas where my middle child learned to walk. We've been to Washington, D.C. where we explored the history of our country. New York City was an exciting trip, too. Disneyland, Disney World, the beaches of the south and of the west coast, the mountains of north Georgia, North Carolina, Colorado skiing—we've been everywhere!

It seems that each trip is an adventure with God and those you love the most. They present an opportunity to see things that we don't see in our ordinary day, sometimes presenting challenges that bond us closer to each other and to God. It would be important to note here that a trip can be a refreshing time together or an exhausting ordeal. The results of a family trip can often be determined by the amount of preparation spent planning and praying for the trip ahead of time.

The main ingredient in successful travel with your family is God. Ask the question, *Is God in this?* If the answer is yes, He will make the experience sweeter than you can imagine! I've been on a few trips that God really didn't intend for me to take. I've learned to ask Him first to guide my steps on everything. If God doesn't want me to travel to a particular place at a particular time, I definitely don't want to go on my own!

I think of Paul in the New Testament and how desperately he dreamed of traveling to Rome and witnessing to the Romans. This burned in his soul, but was not God's plan for him. It took Paul's being imprisoned and chained to settle him enough to complete the New Testament. Through the trial of imprisonment came the blessing of the Word. In all our travels, it is important to ask God, *Is this where You want us to travel and is this the time to go?* He will always answer and if we trust Him to open or close doors, He will.

Traveling with children always adds a little element of surprise and, shall I say, wonder to each trip. Packing with kids is always a hoot! No matter where we are going, we always take too much and come back needing more luggage. On a recent trip to visit family in Georgia, we were detained in the Atlanta airport for having too much luggage and for inspection of the toy Jeep that my parents bought for my oldest son, Davis. I stood for a good forty minutes watching a security team examine and disassemble my son's toy army Jeep. It wasn't so funny at the time as we were about to miss our flight, but we can laugh about it now. (Those last minute trips to Toys-R-Us by the grandparents can be hazardous!)

When you are packing the kitchen sink, remember some first-aid items and your health insurance card. We've spent some time in medical clinics and emergency rooms, too. On one trip to Disney World, Hamilton came down with a fever. He and I took a cab to a nearby clinic while my husband graciously volunteered to take our other son to the park for the day. On a ski trip to Colorado, my son was hit in the head by an icicle about thirty minutes after our arrival and required sutures in the emergency room. On that same trip, our friend fell while skiing and broke his thumb. On the cruise to the Bahamas, I put sea sickness patches on my children who turned the brightest shade of red I have ever seen. I thought I had seriously damaged my children! These are just a few of our experiences with illness or injury while traveling.

The thing I have learned about traveling with my kids is: Expect the unexpected and pray hard before you leave. You can plan and prepare and do everything you know to do to make the trip pleasurable for all, but when it comes down to it, you don't know exactly what's going to happen. That's why you are going on an adventure in the first place! I laugh at how meticulously I prepare for a plane flight with my kids. I've taken bottles, snacks of every kind, and games—Play-Dough, Game Boys, books, coloring books, movies for the computer.... You name it, we take it, including Benedryl (recommended by my pediatrician father).

It never fails, however, that somewhere around the third hour of being in a two-foot by two-foot space, the baby has suddenly had enough! Usually about the time we land, the pressure gets to their ears and they begin to cry...really loud. Not even gum or sippy cups will comfort at this point.

One such flight with our youngest son almost wound up a disaster. Truett was crying as we were landing; nothing would comfort him. The two women sitting in front of us were not amused and kept turning around, giving me the evil eye through the crack between the seats. I was wrestling with this out-of-control two-year-old in my lap, trying to comfort him and keep him quiet out of respect to those around us. But about the fifth time the lady turned around to give me another disapproving look, I had had enough. I lost it, right there on the airplane. I said through the crack between the seats, "I'll bet you did the same thing to your mother when you were this age!"

Well, friends, that put the quietness on the situation! She turned herself around and never looked back again. My husband, watching from across the aisle, was rather amused. He was seated next to an older woman who leaned to him and said, "Never mess with a mother and crying two-year-old!"

How a mother is supposed to keep children from making any noise on a four-hour flight in a space the size of a small box is beyond me! America (as Bernie Mac would say), have a little compassion on our mothers with children on an airplane. You were a baby once, too, you know!

As I thought more about the woman so annoyed in front of me, it never occurred to me that just maybe God had wanted me to pray for her, or that maybe she was going through something and needed a word of encouragement. Maybe all of our travels are not really all about us. Maybe He has a mission for us, a person to reach out to.

We began this chapter with Romans 1:10-11 in which Paul says to pray that he would have a safe trip, and that when he arrived, he would impart something to them. If we and our children could see the journeys that God blesses us with as a mission from Him and to be on the lookout for ministry opportunities, we would be traveling with the heart of God.

Take a moment to record a travel memory with your family.

____

____

____

____

____

____

____

Record a time when God used you or your children to minister to someone on a trip.

____

____

____

____

____

____

____

A Mother's Prayer

Father God, we thank You for giving us the privilege of travel and adventure with our children. We thank You for this beautiful world You have given us to enjoy and explore together. We give You praise and glory for all the opportunities You have given us to travel and to get a glimpse of Your vast creation.

Thank You, God, for Your words in Romans that we have prosperous journeys and that we are able, by Your Holy Spirit, to impart to others Your love and faithfulness along the way. We pray that each trip we take is assigned and appointed by You. We believe that You will give us safety and success in all our travels. We rest in the promise that we are covered by His blood and surrounded by angels as we make our journey. I bless my children's travels near or far, all their days.

In Jesus' name I pray. Amen.

CHAPTER 7

THE MARVELOUS MADNESS OF MEALTIME WITH CHILDREN

Thy wife shall be as a fruitful vine by the sides of thine house: thy children like olive plants round about thy table. Psalm 128:3

The table has been set. The glasses are filled. The TV has been turned off. The meal has been served. I'm feeling quite certain that my family is *really* going to enjoy this meal more than any other before. We've filled everyone's plates and are beginning to sit down when all of a sudden, the phone rings.

"Don't answer it!" my husband says in a loud authoritative tone, almost in slow motion.

"Oops, too late," says my oldest son as he has already jumped for the phone and answered it. "It's for you, Mom," he says, holding the phone out for me.

"Great," I grumble as I wipe mashed potatoes off my hand and make my way to the phone. As I answer I realize it is a sales call and my frustration level goes up. Now while I'm distracted on the phone with a call I didn't want from someone who wouldn't even give me a chance to say hello, I watch as the food gets cold and a fight breaks out between my two boys over a toy. They are in a wrestling match on the floor beneath me and I am trying to excuse myself from the phone over their screams.

Finally freed from the phone, I turn toward the kitchen to see that our two-year-old is now standing in the middle of the table dumping out the salt and pepper. I am beginning to boil inside, feeling that a couple of hours' effort in the kitchen are about to be completely ruined and it is all the kids' fault. As I hang up the phone, break up the fight and begin to clean up the salt and pepper mess, I discipline (nice wording for *yell at*) my children for their behavior. I realize that I don't even want to eat anymore.

My husband and I continue on toward our goal of having a nightly meal together as a family and he says, "I told you we should not answer the phone."

"Yes, I know that," I snip back, ready to hit someone with a spatula.

We get everyone seated and served, always our children's plates first because, by this point, you do not tell a hungry two-year-old to wait. Finally, my husband and I have our plates served, too, and we sit down with a big deep breath. We reach out our hands to hold each other's and say the blessing.

Hamilton starts it and Truett screams, "No! I say it!"

Hamilton whines back, "But I never get to say it."

Finally, my husband says, "Hamilton, let Truett (the baby) say it. You can say it tomorrow." (Of course, that's what he said last night.)

Truett takes his own reverent time saying the blessing, really slowly. "God…is… gracious. God…is…good. Let…us…kank… Him…for…our…food. A…men."

Then we all say amen, to which the baby objects loudly, "No! You not say amen. I say amen!" Then he starts the prayer all over again. "God…is…gracious…."

The other boys start snickering as their dad glares around the table as if to say, "I dare any of you to say amen."

By now the food I had worked on so hard and was so proud of is completely cold. It really doesn't matter to the children who don't notice whether it's hot or cold. As my husband and I are just picking up our forks, our oldest (who usually finishes his drink before we have served our plate) says, "I need more tea."

Knowing he just couldn't possibly eat his meal without another glass of drink, I huff and puff my way to pour him another. As soon as I am seated and my very first bite is almost in my mouth, Hamilton decides he wants more bread. He gets up and goes toward the kitchen. As we are cutting up the children's food, it is a few seconds before my husband and I realize that Hamilton is wandering around in the family room with a toy.

"Get back over here, Hamilton," my husband says. "What do you think you're doing? We're trying to eat here. No one excused you from the table."

"O…K…" Hamilton grumbles as he makes his way back to the table. "But I'm not hungry and my stomach is hurting. I feel like I'm going to throw up!"

At this point, I'm thinking that my stomach is hurting, too. All of a sudden the baby stands up in his seat and announces, "I through!"

Standing there in a diaper with food from head to toe, he's a mess. I plead with him, "Please, please sit down. Daddy and I are just starting to eat." It's useless. Realizing that he is going to persist until we pick him up, I give in, thinking *I can't eat anyway with him standing there covered in food.* So, I start the icky process of cleaning him off, taking him to the sink to "wash him down."

Meanwhile, the other boys are asking to be excused also, to which my husband and I reply in one voice, "No way!"

"We haven't even eaten," we say.

"Yeah," says Hamilton, "and you haven't even asked us about our day, yet."

"You're right," we say, feeling an odd sense of guilt now. We then begin our routine of asking, "What was the happiest thing that happened to you today?"

Trying to make our way through our meal, the boys each share the things that happened during their day. Then they ask to leave the table with a programmed, "May I be excused? I enjoyed it." I'm thinking to myself, *Did we even eat? If so, what did we have?*

Everyone seems to scurry off in different directions and I am left at the table alone, looking around at the aftermath of the meal on the table, the floor, the stove, the sink, and the counters. From the appraisal of it all, it looks like an estimated hour and a half clean-up job...which took only minutes to eat.

I close my eyes, take a deep breath, and try to remember just how fortunate I am to have children around my table. I am blessed to watch them grow each day into the men of God I know they are called to be. Blessed to hear their laughter and chatter as we eat. Blessed to have food to feed them. Blessed to have those dirty pots and pans to wash. My life is truly overflowing with the blessing of God. I am living, breathing, and realizing that I am in God's overflow of blessing. I am experiencing each day the truth of Psalm 128:3, that my sons are like olive branches around my table and that God is good.

Several years ago our marriage pastor preached a profound message on this very verse. In it he pointed out that olives are a sign of richness and that fruit is a sign of blessing. Even though children may exasperate us to no end at the dinner table, I keep that Scripture in the back of my mind. Children are absolutely, without a doubt, evidence of God's rich treasure in our lives. And we as mothers are to be the fruitful vines producing the good fruit of praise and thanksgiving in our homes.

Mealtime is an important and vital time for a family. It is said that one-third of families in America actually sit and eat with each other each week.[1] The dinner table can be a place of happiness, laughter, and great memories. There is a sign which once hung in my kitchen. It read *Apothecary* and I placed it there to remind me of the anointing oil that was made in Exodus 30, symbolic of the healing presence of the Holy Spirit.

In all the chaos that can be in my home, I want the Holy Spirit to come and dine with us, to bring His sweet presence and His peace. We need Him in the everyday moments of life, like when we're trying to have a family meal. The Bible clearly describes Jesus as One who loved to dine with His disciples and friends. I believe the Holy Spirit desires that fellowship with us today.

In order to have that fellowship at the table, I would like to suggest several guidelines to make your family's mealtime happy and enjoyable for all.

1. Invite the Holy Spirit to join your family at mealtime.

Begin each meal with a blessing and prayer of thanks, inviting the Holy Spirit to take His place at the head of your table first. If

---

1. Dr. James Dobson, *Bringing Up Boys* (Carol Stream: Tyndale House, 2005) 92.

ever there were two important times in a family, they would be mealtime and church time. And if there were ever going to be times when the enemy would like to bring in strife, conflict and confusion, it would be at these two times.

I cannot tell you the number of times that, just before the meal, WWIII breaks out. Finally I got a revelation that it was just not coincidence that someone starts a major argument right before we are going to sit down to eat or are on the way to church. Now that I realize this, I say to my children, "Boys, what are the two important times for our family that we get along and don't start fights?"

And they get that "Here-she-goes-again" look in their eyes and reply almost robotically and in unison, "Mealtime and church time." I know my constant teaching may get tiring for them, but I want them to get it through their little heads that no one is messing with our mealtimes!

Join me in this for a moment, girls! All that work to prepare a nice meal, to be, in mere seconds, turned into fight night over something like a toy! Okay, enough said. I'm ranting now.... It's so important to keep these two times as peaceful and as pleasant as possible. Invite the Holy Spirit to join you. He brings peace, comfort and unity.

2. Turn off the TV and don't answer the phone.

If the enemy can get a foot in the door to bring strife at the dinner table, it is also likely to come through an unwelcome or untimely phone call or in a bombardment of negative and depressing TV programs like the evening news. Trying to eat dinner these days while watching the evening news is just asking for indigestion! I highly recommend turning off the TV while eating.

When I would visit Grandmother's house, you could always tell when company was coming by the plume of dust that arose on the dirt road in front of her farm house. Whenever she saw the plume she would say, "Company's coming," and she would turn off the TV and get ready to greet them at the door. By turning off the TV, my grandmother was saying to her company, "I value you and you are important." She was communicating to her guest, "What you have to say is of interest to me and I don't want to hear it over the noise of the television." She had a gift of making everyone feel as if they were the most important person in the world.

By giving one another our undivided attention at the dinner table without the competition of TV and phone, we are communicating to one another (just like Grandmother did), "You are important and I value this time we have together."

3. As often as you can, have everyone start eating at the same time.

Teaching children to wait until everyone is seated with the meal served and the blessing said is one small way to model respect. I know that many families have different traditions, and for some it is perfectly acceptable for the children to be finished with their meal by the time the parents get started. But after many years of trial and error, I have found that what is best for our family (and maybe for yours, too) is for us all to make an effort to eat together and to actually share the meal together.

Acts 2:42 says that the believers continued *steadfastly* in the apostles' doctrine and fellowship, and in breaking of bread, and in prayer. The breaking of bread together was considered a spiritual act of devotion to God and to one another. It symbolized covenant. Meals were meant to be enjoyed together as a time of fellowship, love and communication. Through the act of sitting down together and eating at the same time, you literally bond together as a family.

4. Everyone stays seated until everyone is finished eating.

I am trying to picture Jesus at the last supper, taking His last bite and saying to the disciples as they are trying to finish, "Well boys, I'm finished, so I'm leaving." Not a chance with Jesus! There wasn't a selfish bone in Him. With Him, it was all about others and about pouring into their lives so they could be all they could be. He was all about spending time developing and loving the people closest to Him. What a model of perfect love and of how we should live our lives, beginning in our homes.

In Acts 20, there is another example of the importance of breaking bread together. The disciples had come together over a meal. As they ate, Paul began to preach. The Bible recounts that Paul preached so long at the table that a young man fell asleep, fell out the window and died. That's an awfully long time to stay at the table, don't you think! Well, I'm not suggesting that we stay that long at the dinner table, but let's at least teach our children to show the courtesy toward the person who has prepared and served the meal by staying seated until she/he has finished. (Hopefully they won't fall asleep and fall out of their chairs in the process!) The point of finishing together is that it causes children to slow down and to enjoy their food and fellowship with the family.

Especially in America, we have lost the wonderful art of dining for fellowship and enjoyment. We've traded quiet suppers at home for noisy restaurants and fast food. We no longer value lingering over a peaceful meal together with someone we love. Children are so conditioned to rush, rush, rush. I even find myself saying, "Hurry! Hurry!" many times during the day. Is it any wonder that they want to rush through a meal and get on to the next activity? Finishing the meal together and clearing the table as a family should be one of the most treasured times of our day. So, slow down and enjoy it!

5. Give everyone an opportunity to take turns and share something happy about their day.

This is a tradition we began some years ago in our home when our children started going to school. What I have found, especially with boys, is that when you ask for information about their day, it can be very—shall we say—sketchy. They just don't really spend a lot of time on the details which would give a better picture of how things are *really* going in school.

For instance, I would say, "How was your day?" The response would come, "Good." Then in frustration I would say, "Well, what was your favorite part of the day?" The response I would get would be something like, "P.E.," followed by dead silence.

Okay, I knew I needed a different approach. So, I began to ask the question around the dinner table, one child at a time. "What was the happiest thing that happened to you today?" Then my husband and I would ask, "What was the most challenging or difficult thing that happened today?" And wow! What an interesting response that brought!

All of a sudden, we had details! Details about their life and their friendships and their teachers and their feelings, their struggles. They even revealed the areas where our intervention was required! After discovering that these questions prompted real answers, I felt we had really crossed a milestone in communication with our children. Mealtime is a great time to find out things about your child and his/her interests that maybe you didn't know before.

You see, when you take into account all the wonderful things a child can learn from this very vital hour called mealtime, I think more of us would make breaking bread together a priority. Family mealtimes offers an opportunity to develop vital skills and attitudes that will stay with a child throughout life. These skills include things like gratitude toward God for the meal, respect, manners, communications, obedience, fellowship, sharing, helping and so much more.

As I write this, it is nearing 6:00 PM. That means "suppertime" at our house. I think I'll get everyone to the table and enjoy!

Write down some ways that you can improve your mealtime in order to make it a more pleasurable time for you and your family.

____

____

____

____

____

____

____

What are some habits or traits about your mealtime that need changing or improvement?

____

____

____

____

____

____

____

A Mother's Prayer

Father God, I thank You for the wonderful example You set of breaking bread together. What a privilege it is to be seated together as a family and share a meal. Help me to remember to be grateful at times when our meals seem chaotic and hurried due to the busy-ness of life. Help me to slow down, chew my food, and to remind my children to do the same.

Thank You, God, for Your provision of food and for Your faithful promise that the seed of the righteous will not have to beg for bread. Thank You, God, for making every meal we eat together a happy time so that sweet memories will fill the minds and hearts of my children. Make our mealtime together a time of laughter and joy and make our table a place of healing and love for all who come to enjoy and feast in Your presence.

I speak a blessing over my children that they will be blessed with good food, good mealtimes, and good memories around the table.

In Jesus' name I pray. Amen

CHAPTER 8

THE MARVELOUS MADNESS OF EATING OUT WITH CHILDREN

Among whom also we all had our conversation in times past in the lusts of our flesh, fulfilling the desires of the flesh and of the mind, and were by nature the children of wrath, even as others. Ephesians 2:3

Have you ever been through a time in your life when you lost something and then you gradually began to get it back? If so, then you know that when God restores something in your life, you appreciate it all the more.

This would be our experience with eating out with children. When my older two sons were small, my husband and I seemed to think we had oodles of discretionary income and were able to eat out pretty regularly...okay, a lot! After a move, a financial crisis, and a pay cut, eating out became a rarity. Prior to this hard-knock wisdom we received from God, we would plop down casually at a restaurant after church with friends, order whatever we wanted (including dessert), and then pull out the old "plastic" to pay. We didn't think anything of spending on one meal what most families (including my own) budgeted for several days' groceries.

We really took the whole eating out experience for granted, never once realizing what an incredible privilege it is to take an entire family out to a sit-down meal together. Oh, we said the blessing and we openly gave thanks to God over our meals, but deep down inside we had no clue as to how special it was.

Now I am happy to say that times have changed and God has worked true gratitude in our hearts for the dining out experiences. Recently, my husband's company gave him a little cash bonus. He immediately thought, *let's take this money and take the boys out after church for a nice meal.* We decided that we would go to a family-friendly restaurant that was a little nicer than the usual places we had always taken them before. It was an exciting and special time for our family.

As we slipped into the nice large booth together, I felt so thankful that God had blessed us with the ability to experience this time together. My children were appreciative, but maybe didn't quite share the enthusiasm I had about being blessed with this meal in this nice restaurant. Not that many years earlier, we would have eaten there with no thought of how special or inspiring it was.

It was a wonderful and happy time together. We only had a few forks and spoons drop to the floor. Minimal amounts of food were spilled on the booth and our clothes. And our two-year-old only crawled up on the back of the seat five or six times to peek over at the people behind us! The two older boys, even though there was not a children's menu, were able to settle on ordering a meal that didn't break the bank. And no one threw up! All in all, it was a fantastic experience!

I can remember so many meals eaten out when our children were younger and surviving all kinds of fiascos like dirty diapers just as the waitress served us. One child had a problem with projectile vomiting at any given moment during a meal. This lasted even up into his grade school years. Can you imagine paying for a meal that you and the baby had to wear out of the restaurant? Forgive me for being so candid about these experiences, but only a seasoned mom (and dad) can truly appreciate and understand what I am saying here. Only a mother will hold out her hand to catch when her baby is spitting up.

There have been meals out when one of my children stood up in the high chair and fell out, hitting his head on the floor. There have been fights, spilled drinks, broken plates, and lots of nice tips and apologies to waitresses. I think if I had to do it all over again, I would forego the meals out with small children and save the money for a date night now and then with my husband. I'd feed the kids at home where they are happy and comfortable.

Don't get me wrong. Children do need to have the experience of dining out and learning appropriate manners and skills for eating in public. And I know that sometimes, like when you travel, it is unavoidable. But I believe we should not allow eating out to become a daily habit or allow it to be taken for granted.

Recently my husband and I had a meal at a French restaurant. Soon after we were seated, a little family came in with a baby and a toddler. It was a fairly expensive restaurant, so Edward and I shared a meal. There was no children's menu and the parents of these two young children were searching for something their little ones could eat. The little girl was not very happy when her dad tried to put her in the high chair. She began crying and kicking (been there, done that). Pretty soon, all the crying seemed to upset the roomful of seasoned haute cuisine patrons whose greatest concern was trying to decide what wine to pair with their meal.

For me, I have to ask the question: Why try to eat in a nice restaurant with a baby? Why put yourself through the torment of that, and then pay for it? If you don't have to take small children out to restaurants on a regular basis, save your money and wait until they are older. Then you can all enjoy it together. End of advice!

Another change that God has worked in my heart over the last three years is directly related to our work in our Adopt-a-Block program at church where we help feed and minister to homeless and underprivileged in our city. I can remember eating our anniversary dinner at a restaurant where all the vegetables were *a la carte.* I'm not sure, but I believe in English this means *beware of the price*! We decided to split one of their very large baked potatoes which cost seven dollars. As I sat there eating that dry half of my baked potato, I began thinking of just how many bags of potatoes I could buy for seven dollars and how many of our homeless men and women we could serve a baked potato to for that. I could see their faces as we served them a nice hot potato all wrapped in foil along with all the trimmings. I envisioned how much they would enjoy and appreciate every bite.

These thoughts were almost more than I could handle as I sat there and tried to enjoy our expensive meal that someone had given us as a gift. I almost got mad at myself for not being able to enjoy and receive the blessing that God had given us. My point is this: Eating out is an expensive privilege whether it's fast food, take-out, or sit-down. At the end of the month, the cost adds up!

I am not saying it's wrong to eat out. I am saying that it is special. Drive by any restaurant row in any city on a Friday or Saturday night. Most of them have an hour or so waiting list for seating; dining out in America has become a god. Eating out is a privilege to be enjoyed with moderation. When we forget this and allow our children to forget it, we are in need of a heart checkup. There are families out there who can only dream of having nice clean clothes to wear, of walking into a nice restaurant, and of having the money to pay for a nice meal to enjoy together.

One of the families on our block lives in a filthy, one-bedroom duplex surrounded by crack houses and violence. Neither the father nor the mother works right now, so most of the food they eat comes from the program at church. Recently their home flooded with rain. The carpet had to be taken out. Clothes and dirty dishes were everywhere. Everything was quite a mess.

Somehow, the father got the two small children dressed the best he could, got on our church bus and brought them to church. They sat with our little family during the service. I was so moved by the little three-year-old girl as she raised her hands upward to heaven as we sang praise songs. All of us—including her father—were overcome by her fervency of spirit and praise.

At the end of the service, he took the children, slipped out of the row of seats, and ran to the altar before the altar call was even given. Without a divine intervention these little children would not know the privilege of clean clothes or hot meals, let alone enjoying a nice restaurant.

If eating out has become an everyday thing, not a big deal to you and your family, maybe it's time to have a few meals at home. Eat a few sandwiches after church or return to some peanut butter and jelly. Maybe we all could use some "humble pie" every now and then. Then make eating out a special event. Let's teach our children that it's a privilege. Your family will enjoy and appreciate your dining out experiences so much more.

What are some ways you can be better stewards of your "eating out" budget?

____

____

____

How can you instill in your child a gratitude for the opportunity and privilege of eating out?

A Mother's Prayer

Father God, we are so grateful for Your incredible provision to enjoy life to the fullest. We are thankful for the privilege of being able to walk into restaurants and enjoy meals together from time to time. Help us to remember that this is a blessing and to never take it for granted. Help us to remember the countless families in our world who can only dream of the opportunity to eat out. Give us hearts of compassion for those who need Your love and allow us to make a difference in our world as stated in Jude 2. Help us not to be selfish with the blessings You give us, especially in eating out.

Help us to seek out those You would have us bless with a nice dinner. Make us ever mindful that it is more blessed to give than to receive and to be conduits of Your love and abundance wherever we go.

Help me as a mother to model the Spirit of Christ and generosity to others for my children's sake. I speak a blessing over my children that they prosper in all areas of their life to bless their families and others.

In Jesus' name I pray. Amen.

CHAPTER 9

THE MARVELOUS MADNESS OF MINISTRY WITH CHILDREN

Let no man despise thy youth; but be thou an example of the believers, in word, in conversation, in charity, in spirit, in faith, in purity. 1 Timothy 4:12

A friend of mine once said jokingly, "I can do anything I need to do with my children alongside. It just takes five times as long." I've laughed about that comment many times as we set out to serve God in our church.

As I mentioned in the previous chapter, we serve as block pastors to several blocks in our inner city and have been asked to do many other jobs as laymen in our church. There are so many happy memories of serving God together as a family, I couldn't begin to count them all.

Easy? Not always. Rewarding? Absolutely! The hours we have invested into God's kingdom, doing His work, we count as treasures laid up in heaven. We wouldn't trade them for anything in this world. There is nothing more satisfying in life than serving God together as a family. We are thrilled to be counted worthy of the cause of serving Christ.

Some of those memories of working together with our children include teaching Sunday school classes, Saturday morning's Adopt-a-Block, collecting turkeys for the Thanksgiving give-away, and putting bicycles together for Christmas gifts, to name just a few. There are plenty of ministries we can all serve in as parents with our children and FOR our children. How about teaching your toddler's class? Think of the joy you can experience by pouring into those children's lives and watching your own child interact and make new friends! Our church requests that we serve one service each month. That is a small amount of time to serve for the blessing it can bring back to you.

Learning how to balance ministry and family has become a way of life for us. After our children were first born, I can remember quickly nursing them in the gymnasium bathroom of our church just before leading a Sunday school class. Many times I had to clean spit-up off my dress before class. There were Sundays we would have to buy complete new outfits for the baby at one of the few stores open before church as we had already gone through the extra outfits packed in the diaper bag. Yes, it was frustrating at the time, but looking back on it, I wouldn't trade the experience of serving together as a family.

We have had so many great blessings in ministry—like serving with our children on Adopt-a-Block. There is no doubt that our family, and hopefully our generations, will be changed forever. Let me share with you how it all got started.

We began this new chapter of life and ministry several years ago when our youngest was about five weeks old. Having just gone through a very painful trial, we knew that we had to do something to get our minds off our problems and focus on the needs of others. For a small town girl from rural South Georgia, it took all the courage I could muster to attend that first Saturday morning meeting and hit the "mean" hot streets of one of the most drug-infested areas of Phoenix.

I tried to talk myself out of it, and on the way in, stopped to ask a woman if I could bring a baby out to do Adopt-a-Block. She quickly replied that there was no way she would ever bring a baby out to do this work. After hearing this, I was elated! I thought to myself, *well now, there's my out! I told You, God, this was not a good idea!*

Nevertheless, I decided to at least go into the meeting to hear what it was all about. At the meeting there were some brief testimonies from the other leaders and block pastors. There was a short teaching from the pastor over the program. After hearing an inspiring word and seeing the love and real Spirit of Jesus Christ in that room, I knew that this was where I wanted to be in order to grow and to learn. We had found our place! And even though I had been discouraged from bringing my children, we decided to try it anyway and trust God to give us safety, the energy and the desire to go out together.

That was nearly four years ago and we've continued, by the grace of God, to go out as a family and minister to the homeless, the prostitutes, the crack addicts, the oppressed and the hungry. We've missed a few Saturdays, and some days we've gone when we just really didn't have the desire to be there, but every time we have gone, we have come away with more blessings than what we gave out!

We began slowly, by taking our new baby out with a team that ministers and feeds the homeless in the park. It was difficult at first because I was a pediatrician's daughter and working in hospitals was my career. I knew all about germs and the dangers they can pose to a small baby. I took a lot of criticism from people who didn't feel I should have my children out ministering. The homeless, in particular, wanted to hold the baby and touch him. I think that the promise of new life brought a hope to them that they had lost sight of. As Truett got older and began to know and recognize the people on the street that we ministered to, he wanted to go to them to be held or to give them a hug. Let me add that we take a lot of precautions physically and spiritually to ensure the safety of our family and children.

One homeless man stands out in my mind. He was an older man with white hair and a beard. He was usually covered with dirt and he just loved Truett. And Truett loved him! There was a playground there in the park and sometimes, under close supervision, he would push Truett in the swing. One day when Truett was almost two, this man decided he wanted to take Truett down the "curly" slide. Can you picture it? This seventy-year-old homeless man going down the slide with my baby! I was about to have a stroke over it and asked several of our team to stay right with him at all times.

Crazy mother! I hear some of you thinking! But do you know that I felt that Truett, even in his youth, was somehow ministering to this man the love of Christ. During that time, this man really connected to our family and began coming to church on a regular basis. On special Sundays like Christmas and our bike give-away, he would ride the bus in with us and stay with me to help out the entire morning. People would stare like *what is that woman doing with that homeless man!*

Once, one of our leaders who has a powerful ministry to the homeless brought this man to our regular Saturday morning Adopt-a-Block meeting. The old man decided to sit with our family on the back row. In a half-drunken stupor, he kept asking me out loud, "You do this every Saturday?"

"Shh," I would say. "Pastor is speaking."

Shaking his head, he would continue really loudly, "What, are you crazy or something? Every Saturday?"

Sitting there listening to him, I began to think *maybe we are crazy; I don't know.*

Even though he is still on the streets and we've lost track of him now, I have to believe that somehow we sowed some eternal seeds into his life and that he will never be the same. I am ever reminded of the Scripture in Matthew 25:40 where Jesus said, *Inasmuch as ye have done it unto one of the least of these my brethren, ye have done it unto me.* What an amazing passage! What an amazing promise!

Charles Spurgeon in his devotional, *Morning by Morning,* wrote of this Scripture:

> *Surely this assurance is sweet enough, and this motive strong enough to lead us to help others with a willing hand and a loving heart—remembering that all we do for His people is graciously accepted by Christ as done to Himself.*[1]

We met a prostitute living in a crack house on one of the blocks we ministered to. This home was run by a man who supplied much of the neighborhood with drugs. But despite all of the business activity coming and going, he didn't manage to pay his water or light bill. So, here we have a home occupied by lots of people, but without running water or electricity. That means that there was no air conditioning—this was Phoenix in 110-degree heat! The things we witnessed just in our Saturday visits to that home over the course of a year before it was finally condemned are unspeakable.

But then, once again, it was my children who really opened the door to those hardened hearts to receive the love of Jesus and the message of the gospel. When the lady would see our van drive up, she would run out of the house—barefooted on the hot pavement, hair matted, body frail and dirty, waving her hands in the air (which

1. Charles Spurgeon, *Morning by Morning* (New Kensington:Whitaker House, 2001).

incidentally were missing several fingers after having them blown off by crack pipe accidents). She would be so excited and I will always remember her saying, "My babies! My babies!" as she rushed out to see our boys. For just that brief moment, I could see real joy and a big smile on her face as she came to greet the children. It wasn't Edward or me she was excited to see, or the other adults on the team or even the food. It was the children!

One day the boldness of the Holy Spirit came over our oldest son, Davis, and he asked her if she had Jesus in her heart. We stood together on the street corner that hot summer day and led her in the prayer of salvation. Later that week, she turned herself in for several warrants and has been incarcerated ever since. We've never been able to find out where she is. We continue to think of her and pray for her that she will get the spiritual teaching and support she needs in prison.

We also had the chance to pray with the crack dealer who lived there. He prayed the salvation prayer right there in the front yard. Our team, including the children, continued to pray that God would remove the crack house from the neighborhood. Sure enough, about a year later, it closed! Peace has come back into that block. Think of that! Hundreds of homes and lives were made better because of the prayers and ministry of a child!

With our own eyes we have witnessed countless examples like this—the ministry of children and their effectiveness in doing the work of God! Now on our blocks, we have begun asking God to lead us to children who will get saved, start coming on the bus to church, and get on fire for the things of God. We have even prayed for some of them to take on the responsibility of "children block pastors" in their neighborhoods. This is a role they take very seriously.

Our prayer and deacon leader once brought a prayer team out to our area, walking the streets and praying over many of our children. Now, those same children are going out and inviting their friends and families to come to church and they are becoming Christians. Amazing! It's an entire revival sparked by children!

When speaking to Timothy, a young minister of the gospel, Paul admonished him to be true to the calling of God on his life. He told him clearly not to be intimidated by others because he was young (See 1 Tim. 4:12). As a mother I try to remind myself of this when out on the urban mission field with my children. Though their physical bodies be small, the spirit man within, having been fed and nourished with the Word of God, is large! And the effect they can have on lives for the kingdom of God is phenomenal!

I think of the thousands of children who serve on the mission fields of the world with their parents. One of my most beautiful friends had her first child—a baby girl— while serving as a missionary in Korea. She reminds us all of the vast work for God that must be done in our world. I marvel at my minister and pastor friends who have children. They demonstrate the grace God gives by being incredible parents while serving God and teaching their children to minister as well.

Paul told Timothy to not let anyone despise his youth, but rather be an example. Children will be an example if we give them the respect, the freedom, and the training they need to become all they can be for Christ. Yes, it may be difficult. Yes, it is hard to organize a ministry team, load up food for ten or more families, and keep an eye on my children all at the same time! Yes, it is difficult to serve in ministry while being true to my first call of being a wife and a mother. But when we allow God to lead us, He can take our "little" efforts and multiply them.

As I have written this chapter, I have been interrupted almost every five minutes with a houseful of children and summertime blues! Truett has stopped my writing several times to give me an explanation about how the devil used to be an angel with pretty wings. All the children have come into the kitchen where I've been writing—numerous times—and opened the freezer so much that the popsicles have melted all over the floor. How's a girl to think?

My friend's comment about it taking five times as long to complete a project with your children is somewhat accurate. Yes, living a life for God and serving Him with your children alongside is challenging. But, oh, how much richer, more meaningful, and exciting children make the journey when we learn to serve together and allow the Holy Spirit to teach us through them!

Think of some ways you can include your children in God's work in your church and community.

____

____

____

____

____

Record some spiritual truths and treasures you have learned from your children or the children of others.

____

____

____

____

____

____

A Mother's Prayer

Father God, I thank You for Your Word that says, A little child shall lead them (Isa. 11:6). I thank You for the power of Your Holy Spirit which lives and dwells in my children and that they are dedicated to Your work and service. I thank You for the powerful work that they are doing and will do for the furtherance of Your kingdom.

I praise You for their youth and that no man will despise them. I thank You, God, for the great favor You have placed on them and that Your Word dwells in them richly. I ask You to consecrate their work all the days of their life and that through them, millions of lives will be touched and impacted for the glory of God.

I speak a blessing over my children, that the ministry You have given them is and will be effective, powerful, and anointed for Your kingdom.

In Jesus' name I pray. Amen.

CHAPTER 10

THE MARVELOUS MADNESS OF CARING FOR SICK CHILDREN

They that be whole need not a physician, but they that are sick.
Mat. 9:12

Well, there is absolutely nothing marvelous about caring for a sick child. It is painful and frightening, and oh, so draining to see little bodies endure attacks and discomfort. It's especially hard when they are so young and can't communicate; they seem so helpless.

I can remember stomach viruses hitting in the wee hours of the night with no prior warning. Suddenly the whole household is awakened by all the changing of sheets and commotion. As painful a subject as this is, I would be remiss if I didn't address this area of raising and caring for children.

God's Word has much to say about caring for sick children. Elijah was approached by the woman whose son had actually died and she bid the man of God to raise him from the dead. Jesus was approached many times by desperate parents who needed a healing touch on their children.

In the ninth chapter of Matthew, Jesus was approached by a certain ruler whose daughter had died. Jesus was so moved by the pain combined with the worship and faith of this ruler that He followed the father to his home, touched the dead girl and raised her up to life.

What is interesting to me in this story is that the Bible records that the people there at the home of the dead girl laughed Jesus to scorn. His desire to heal this little girl had to press past the unbelief and ridicule of the people around her. That's still true today. Sometimes we must press past the unbelief, ridicule and scorn of even our fellow Christians to see that gift of healing in operation as it should be.

In Luke 18:16 (NKJV) Jesus says, *Let the little children come to Me, and do not forbid them; for of such is the kingdom of God.* The implication here is that some of the children brought to Jesus may have been sick and needed His touch. In this case, it was the disciples who rebuked the people for bringing the children and did not want them to be allowed to come near.

Sometimes we as mothers and parents can be like this, even today. Our child gets sick, begins running a fever, starts other symptoms of coughing or a runny nose, maybe even nausea and vomiting. And what do we do? Do we take them to God first? Do we scorn the idea of praying first and asking God to heal them? Do we treat the symptoms and/or call the doctor...and *then* pray? As parents, this is the dilemma—and what exactly should we do?

I remember as a child there were many dinner meals (supper to me) interrupted by frantic and upset mothers calling my pediatrician dad with questions about their sick children. It wasn't bad enough that I had to give up my dad to many kids in our small town every day (even the weekends), but it was particularly irritating to share him during our family meals. Typically, my dad's end of the conversation went something like this.

"How long has she been running a fever?" "**Three** days!" "Well, honey (my southern dad's name for all mothers and grandmothers of his patients), why haven't you brought her in before now?"

The next questions usually came about the time I was taking a bite of my mother's delicious meatloaf or salmon cakes (popular dishes when I was growing up). They could really put a damper on my appetite.

"Well, is she vomiting?" "Does she have diarrhea?" "Is it watery?" On and on the questions went. My brother and I could almost ask the questions along with dad, using his same tone and inflections—a talent he probably didn't particularly appreciate, but which was quite funny to us. After we got older, we could ask the questions on our own, take down the information, and give it to Dad to call them back *after* the meal!

As a mother, I have had times when the children were sick and I just had no idea what to do. I have called the doctor the moment they spiked a temperature, sat for several hours in the waiting room, paid for the office visit only to be told, "Your child has a cold, and there is nothing we can do but let it run its course."

Then there have been situations when I have decided that I'm not going down there to that office to look like some idiot this time. I'll just treat them myself and wait it out! (Just being honest here.) That's been the time when I finally call the doctor three or four days later and he says, "How many days has your child had a fever?"

"Three," I respond. About that time a wave of guilt comes crashing in, and you feel like the worst mother on the planet!

So, what are parents to do when our children are ill? After years of croupy coughs, high fevers, bumps, bruises, stitches, scratches, dental surgeries, headaches, sinus infections, stomach viruses too numerous to count, growth issues, premature birth, seizures, and more, I can tell you quite honestly—I don't know! The only thing I have found effective to do *every* time and right at first, is to pray.

Pray! Imagine that! It sounds so very simple and so obvious, yet even seasoned Christian moms can get so caught up in the symptoms, the emergency, or the discomfort of our child that we forget. We forget to bring our child to the One and the only One who is the true source of healing in every case, every time, anywhere.

Pray and ask God for wisdom to know what to do. James 5:16 says, *...the effectual fervent prayer of a righteous man* (or woman or mother) *avails much.* This is the very best advice any mother could give a new mom. It is good to be informed and to read everything you can about taking care of a sick child. But when our children are attacked by an illness, we need the wisdom of God. We need supernatural knowledge. We need the gift of healing. And we need these gifts in operation immediately. If we'll just seek first the kingdom and ask, God will reveal whether or not to call the doctor immediately or wait a little while. The Bible teaches us that we have not because we ask not (See James 4:2). If we will ask for the gift of healing, God will give it to us.

One thing is certain. God's heart is for children! He moves on the scene for a child now just as He did when the ruler begged Jesus to come to his home. James 5:14 says, *Is any sick among you? Let him call together the elders of the church and anoint him with oil in the Name of the Lord. And the prayer of faith shall save the sick, and the Lord shall raise him up.*

That's a promise. When I hear a promise, I cling to it and remind God of it. Anointing with oil is not some antiquated religious act that went out of vogue centuries ago. No, to the contrary, it is still just as necessary and important to us today! Maybe along with our first-aid kits, medicine cabinets and purses, we should consider including a small vial of anointing oil to remind us to pray for those in need.

If this sort of thing is new to you, it may seem a little too spiritual. But I can assure you that every time God has led me to pray for someone and anoint them with oil He has not failed to amaze me with His miracle-working power. Who better to pray for and to believe God for healing than our own precious children.

I have some friends who are battling cancer. It has been an excruciating thing for them and for their children and friends. But God has been so faithful to carry them through this journey with great strength and faith. I use the word *journey* because that's how one precious friend describes her fight.

"It is a journey that God has taken me on, and I wouldn't trade the place He has brought me to," my friend says. She is a gift to the body of Christ and an inspiration of what it means to be a beautiful woman of God.

The power of prayer has been so evident in the journey of another of my friends. We sat together as a church and asked God to bring her through the seven-hour surgery to remove a cancerous tumor from her brain. Miraculously, two days later, she was released from the hospital to go home with her husband and boys on Mother's Day!

Another story about God's miraculous healing power took me back to a time when I was a student at Oral Roberts University. A young man came to our Sunday night prayer meeting requesting prayer for healing of cancer. The cancer had been located in his foot and without a miracle, it would be amputated.

This young man had formerly practiced Judaism and had been raised in a Jewish home, but had given his heart to the Lord. After that he decided to attend the same university.

As the chaplain and I placed our hands on that young man's foot and fifty or more students behind us joined in, we prayed the prayer of faith and commanded that cancer to leave his body. As all were fervently praying, I felt a sensation go through my right hand and out the back! When I looked up, the chaplain had obviously experienced the same thing. We were perplexed and amazed, and believed God that this young man had truly been healed.

Several days later, he was scheduled for the surgery at a nearby hospital. Prior to surgery, with his family members waiting in the lobby, the doctors called for one last MRI before amputating the foot. To everyone's total surprise, the MRI came back totally clear! The cancer was gone! The surgery was canceled!

This young man had a strong Christian nurse who went out to report the good news to his family. And right there in that hospital waiting room, she was able to lead them to the Lord! Hallelujah! God had a plan!

In Deuteronomy 11:19-20 we read how Moses commanded the children of Israel to write God's commandments, His ways, upon the doorposts of their homes and upon the hearts of their children. He said to speak about God while eating, while lying down and when rising up. It says to speak of them and teach them.

If we don't exercise our faith and teach our children that God is the healer, who is going to teach them? We first must model the Word at home for our children—that God wants to heal, that He has the power to heal, and that He will heal. He may choose a number of different pathways to healing. He may use the merging of prayer and medicine, as I have seen modeled by my father as he has prayed and laid hands on literally thousands of patients over the years. But we must be the ones to carry this legacy and teaching on to our children and the generations. The gift of healing and the prayer of faith are as relevant and necessary for our families today as they were when Jesus walked the earth.

So, girls, what are we going to do the next time the enemy tries to attack the health of our household? We are going to remember to pray the prayer of faith. We're going to remember to anoint our children, spouse and extended family with oil. We are going to remember to release the healing power of God through the laying on of hands. We are going to remember those thirty-nine stripes that Jesus bore on His back so that our health could be paid for. We are going to bring our children to Jesus and entrust them to His hands, the great Healer, the greatest Physician of all time!

Write about a time when you witnessed the healing power of God. This will encourage your faith. Take a moment to tell your children about this experience.

____

____

____

____

____

List the order of things you want to do when faced with illness in your family. (Example: "I will not fear or panic; I will first…")

____

____

____

____

____

____

A Mother's Prayer

Father God, I thank You for Your Word and promise that says that by Jesus' stripes, I am healed (Isa. 53:5). I thank You that I can apply the promise attached to those stripes to my children when they are suffering with illness. I release Your healing power to flow in my children from the tops of their heads to the soles of their feet.

I believe You have come that we may have life and life more abundantly. I ask You to heal my child from any or all diseases or illnesses. I ask that You will cover them by Your blood and protect them from any and all future attacks on their health. We cancel the enemy's assignment to bring sickness, calamity, or accidents on our children.

We believe Your Word, God, that our children will live and not die and declare the works of the Lord. We ask that any iniquity or generational diseases such as diabetes, cancer, heart disease, addictions, mental illness or infirmity of any sort be broken off of our lives and our children's lives and our children's children.

We thank You for health, healing, and wholeness and for the high price You paid on the cross so that we might have it! I speak a blessing over my children's bodies, minds, and spirits that they be healthy and strong and blessed with long life. I declare that my children will live a life of honor and praise.

In the Name of Jesus Christ of Nazareth we pray and believe! Amen.

CHAPTER 11

THE MARVELOUS MADNESS OF RAISING RESPECTFUL CHILDREN

A gracious woman retains honor. Proverbs 11:16

Shortly after moving from Georgia to Arizona, I declared to my family, "I will give up the beautiful azaleas that bloom in the spring. I will give up the magnolia trees which grace the landscape of South Georgia. I will give up the creeks, rivers, and waterfalls I have become so accustomed to. I will think about giving up sweet tea (something I've yet to do). I will consider giving up grits almost every day. I will give up the wonderful fresh tomatoes, okra and corn. But there is one South Georgia custom I absolutely will not part with; it is non-negotiable." Want to know what it is? It is four little phrases: yes, ma'am; no, ma'am; yes, sir; no, sir.

Now, call me old fashioned if you want to, but this is the one thing I just absolutely insist upon with my children when it comes to responding and addressing an adult. I know that seldom do you hear this anymore and I have been told that some people take offense to it. But I believe that those very small phrases contain a dynamite force—the power of respect.

I was taught to address my elders in this way when I was young, and it is a tradition I hope that will continue for even my great-great grandchildren. My boys respond with it pretty regularly—many times with a reminder—and I am pleased to say that most people have responded favorably to their show of respect. I certainly prefer it to the typical *yeah, nah,* and *huh?* we hear so much today.

Now, I'm not suggesting that everyone must teach their children those same "southern" responses, although our military seem to think they are pretty important, too. I am suggesting that we teach them to at least respond with a *yes, thank you* or *no, thank you* or *yes, please* or *no, please*. A little eye contact is always nice, too. Even a small child can learn to have a firm handshake and look an adult in the eye.

In a recent survey of over 400 men, Harvard graduate Shaunti Feldhahn asked the question, "If you had to choose between having the feelings of being alone and unloved or of being inadequate and disrespected, which would you choose?" An overwhelming response from the men revealed that over seventy percent would choose being alone and unloved over being disrespected.[1]

Now apply that response to our children today, and it is easy to see that there truly is an epidemic of disrespect in our society. Turn on just about any secular TV show and you will find rampant disrespect woven into much of the dialog. What an eye-opener is this recent survey of men and how humbling to note just how respect-deprived many of them in our society are. Great insight and understanding can be gained from this survey, which can help us in our relations with husbands, children, fathers, fathers-in-law, brothers and male peers.

So, just exactly what is respect and how do we teach it to our children? Respect means to show honor to the worthy. To honor is to esteem or regard highly. So important and vital is honor and

1. Shaunti Feldhahn, *For Women Only: What You Need to Know about the Inner Lives of Men* (Sisters: Multnomah Publishers Inc., 2004).

respect that God included it in the ten commandments. The fifth commandment tells us to honor our father and mother. Honor implies obedience to authority and an appreciation for the boundaries that they set in our lives.

There are two things I find myself constantly saying to my children: listen and obey. Here's the reason I do that. If you cannot learn to hear my voice and obey it, how will you ever learn to hear God's still small voice and obey Him? If you don't hear and obey His voice, you are going to have some miserable situations on your hands! Just ask me; I know from personal experience!

In his book *It Is Better to Build Boys than Mend Men* Truett Cathy states, "Children want limits, and they want to be able to respect the adults who set those limits." He goes on to say, "If children have no respect for authority, no amount of punishment is going to change them." [2]

One of the best ways to teach children respect for authority is to model our own adherence to the chain of command. Adults can do this by worshipping and respecting God and by obeying the rules of law. Many of us know people who are living in their own world and we just happen to be living in it. In other words, they could care less about anybody else's life but their own. If I am not careful, I can raise my children to be this way and can model this behavior myself.

Respect incorporates listening, caring, asking questions, and preferring one another. It is in the absence of respect that we breed dysfunction. Most all families at some time or another lack a show of respect and may seem somewhat dysfunctional. I recently joked with my sister about this and in her witty way, she quipped, "Honey, we put the FUN in dysfunction!" We had a great laugh together. Per-

---

2. S. Truett Cathy, *It Is Better to Build Boys than Mend Men* (Looking Glass Books, 2004).

haps many of us feel that we have come through or out of some level of dysfunction. Hey, that's life.

What I am learning is, with the current bend toward sarcasm and disrespect that bombards our children, if we don't make *deliberate* attempts to teach respect, they won't recognize it. With so many opportunities for pleasure, entertainment, and adventure for our kids today, if we don't watch it, we can raise them to be pretty self-absorbed. To converse with some of our kids today, you don't know whether you are watching a TV program of the *The Fabulous Life of…* or talking to a real child.

For me, life seemed much simpler as a child. Much of my summer vacation consisted of working in my grandmother's garden with my mother, dad, brother, sister, cousins, aunts and uncles helping to can our vegetables for the year and working on the farm. If we got all the bushels of peas shelled for the day, we would get to go to the Alapaha River for a swim in the afternoon.

My cousins and I recently reminisced that we don't ever remember having meat from the grocery store when we were growing up. It was always "put up" by our grandparents and families, usually during the Thanksgiving holiday. Our syrup was made right there on the farm during cane grinding season. All of this food preparation was hard word and something about hard work teaches us to respect.

When I was a little older, my dad allowed me to work for him in his doctor's office, which gave me the opportunity to make a little income and to learn some valuable skills for later in life. He put a little lab coat on me and put me to task getting patients into their rooms and ready to be seen.

In high school he taught me how to manage his insurance and Medicare/Medicaid filing. I wouldn't trade my experiences working as a child and teenager for any camp or trip around the world. How could you ask for a more wonderful dad?

Those of us who can, should be willing to teach our children the value of work and some skills for later in life. I don't mean to imply that we never took vacations! And yes, there was time for play and relaxation. But my parents certainly didn't feel the pressure we feel today to enroll us in every camp that came along or jet set ups all over the country.

It is so humbling to think about our Adopt-a-Block kids who only dream about the chance to go swimming just once during the summer. On one of our blocks, we have two families living in a one-bedroom apartment with nine children. Most of these kids didn't have shoes and ran around barefooted on the hot pavement. Their apartments are cooled by swamp coolers, not air conditioning, and they have limited toys and entertainment. Some of the women from church got together and took food, clothes, toys, furniture, games and videos so the children would at least have some activities.

Another child we met there works for his father in landscaping in the heat every day and is one of the most respectful and grateful young men we have ever known. Every day he works in that extreme desert heat to help provide money and food for his family.

Psalm 138:6 says, *Though the Lord be high, yet hath he respect unto the lowly: but the proud he knows afar off.* The older I get, I find myself so drawn to the humble and meek people of the world and less attracted to or impressed by the glamorous and the fabulous. God is developing in me a great respect and compassion for those that I used to disregard or ignore. What I am finding is that respect for the lowly and meek yields great treasure in our life.

I would like to relay one such treasure that God dropped into my lap only recently. Following our Tuesday morning women's Bible study at church, I decided to walk down to our church café where my oldest son was working. As I walked in the door, I noticed a man who appeared to be homeless sitting in one of the chairs with a backpack. A few moments later, a woman came in and bought this man lunch. I watched him as he made several trips to the salad bar and then return to his seat with his head down.

My heart broke for this "young" man and I felt that God would have me talk to him and see what we needed to do to help. I walked over to his table and introduced myself and found out his name. I began the awkward conversation by asking if he knew any of our leaders with the homeless outreach. I asked him if he had been to any of the services here at the church. I noticed that he had two books with him on the table, one of them a Bible, and we talked briefly about those.

I went on to ask him if we could help him connect with our ministry for shelter, discipleship and food. We introduced him to the coordinator of our bus ministry and security staff member who had noticed the man sleeping in our prayer center the night before. I tried to temper the conversation with the greatest care and respect so as not to embarrass or talk down to him, remembering that except for the grace of God, I might be in the same shoes.

Just about the time I was about to walk away from the table, I had the impression that I should ask where he was from. Even as I heard myself asking the question, the most amazing response came out of this man's mouth. "I'm from Georgia," he said with his head down.

"No way!" I responded excitedly. "I am, too! Where in Georgia?"

And with an even quieter, almost embarrassed tone, he replied, "A little town called Tifton."

"Get out of here!" I almost yelled out as I had to pull out a chair and sit down. "I'm from Tifton!"

"Really?" He responded with a bit of a smile.

"Yes, I graduated from Tifton County High," I said.

"I never graduated," he said, lowering his eyes. "The last school I attended was Woodrow Wilson Middle School."

"I went to Woodrow Wilson Middle School, too," I told him. "I lived on Marty Lane near the hospital," I said.

He looked at me and said, "I lived on Twentieth Street near the hospital."

"No way!" I'm yelling at this point with the whole café listening in. "Did you go to Northdale Elementary?"

He nodded his head yes.

"Well, how old are you?" I asked, forgetting all manners at that point.

"I'm forty-two," he replied.

I almost cried. We were the same age! Which meant we had been in the same classes! We had walked the same hallways, played on the same playgrounds and eaten in the same school cafeterias.

We sat in silence for a moment almost too shocked to speak. By this time several people in the café had heard my conversation with this homeless man and were also involved. The woman who bought his lunch started yelling, "This is God (Gawd)! This is God, honey!" She turned to him and said, "This is destiny! This sort of thing doesn't just happen!"

We were in stunned amazement at what had just taken place. A chance encounter three thousand miles away from our hometown with a homeless man I almost disregarded, turned out to be one of the greatest treasured moments of my life. Think of it! I rarely walk down to the café during the day like that, especially when it is so hot.

Many things had to fall into place in order for me to meet this young man. First my husband, who was picking me up at church, was running late. My son, at the last minute, decided to help out at the café that day which prompted my visit. My other two boys begged to stay and eat lunch. And my former childhood classmate, neighbor, fellow South Georgian, the homeless man, did not get work that day so decided to hang out in the café. Amazing! See how precise and accurate and incredible our God is! See how much God loves the ones society calls lowly. See how much He loves you and me and delighted in giving us all that surprise meeting!

Later I called my mom and dad to share with them what had happened. They remembered the family from our small town and my dad remembered seeing some of them as patients.

The greatest and most amazing element in our meeting was in the fact that God had to work into my heart a compassion and respect for those homeless people. Years ago, before I began working with Adopt-a-Block and street ministry with my pastor who lives his life by Jude 2 ("some having compassion, making a difference"), I would never have spoken to a homeless person. I probably would have been annoyed that he was hanging out in "our" café; I would have judged him. Maybe if you caught me on a good day, I would have given him a few dollars to buy a meal, but I never would have considered having a conversation with him. I had absolutely no respect for the meek and lowly, absolutely no regard for the young man or woman who had lost his/her way.

You see, God had to work into my heart a respect for all people. Respect for those with power, success and fame. Respect for my husband. Respect for my parents. Respect for my children. Respect for my pastors and leaders. Respect for people bound by sin (not for the sin, but compassion and respect for the person). And...respect for people with no place to sleep tonight. That chance encounter that day gave me a whole new perspective, which I hope to carry with me as we work with the homeless in the inner city and hope to instill in my children and grandchildren.

That perspective is: every homeless man or woman, every person bound by drugs or alcohol, every prostitute, every prisoner, every sick person you meet is someone's child. They are someone's baby! And they once were a little boy or girl in elementary school—maybe even in your class. They had hopes and dreams for a bright and promising future. After that encounter that day, I will never look at the homeless the same way again.

My children and I prayed with the man in the café and thanked God for the gift of meeting him. Our security officer made some phone calls and found a place for him. We gave him our name and a phone number to call for help. We left that day and said we would be looking for him at church.

As we said goodbye, my three-year-old shook his hand and said, "Nice to meet you, Mister."

"Nice to meet you, too," he replied. "How old are you, son?"

"Three," Truett answered, holding up his fingers.

"Three!" the man said with amazement.

As we turned to leave my child responded with a big smile and in his inherited southern drawl, "Yes, sir."

Right at that very moment, it dawned on me that God *is* teaching me respect. And regardless of the moments when I feel inadequate and guilty of being a terrible mother, and in all the madness that motherhood brings, the Holy Spirit *is* teaching my children through me, and we are living a blessed life because of it.

A gracious woman retains honor. In other words, she keeps honor and respect around her, prevalent in her heart and in her home. My prayer for you and I, dear friend, is that we will be those gracious women who retain and teach honor and respect in our homes.

What changes do you need to implement in your parenting in order to teach the principles of honor, respect, good manners and hard work?

List some specific ways you can begin teaching your children to respect others.

What are some ways you and your family can together show respect and honor to those society might consider lowly and weak?

A Mother's Prayer

Father God, grant me the understanding to know how to show respect to my family. Help me to live and conduct myself as a respectful woman of God. Help me, Lord, to show respect and honor to You, my husband, my children, my parents, my pastors, my leaders, my children's teachers, and all those You allow me to know and serve.

Help me to teach my children through example how to be people who respect others, particularly those who are considered lowly. Thank You, God, for making our lives so much richer when we learn to live within the boundaries of respect and honor You have set. We bless You, Lord, for Your ways are greater and much higher than ours. And there is safety when we walk in obedience to Your Word.

Help me teach my children to love and embrace Your laws. And give me the grace to teach my children to clearly hear Your voice speaking to them, being quick to obey. I speak a blessing over my children that they will be respectful and kind and hard working in all their ways.

In Jesus' name I pray. Amen.

CHAPTER 12

THE MARVELOUS MADNESS OF RAISING CHEERFUL CHILDREN

He that is of a merry heart, has a continual feast. Proverbs 15:15

One of the things I forget to do the most is to play with my kids. If my children could grade me in all areas of motherhood, this would be one of the areas I'd flunk. Too serious about life and often too burdened about cares I shouldn't carry, I forget to have fun and enjoy.

Everything to me has a purpose and a goal. When I go swimming it is to exercise and then hurry to get out. When I am vacationing with my children, I am so focused on making sure everyone is safe and has clean underwear, I forget to enjoy. When I am watching a movie with my children I am usually folding several loads of laundry. When I am spending time with friends in our home, I am usually worrying about making them comfortable, rather than enjoying their presence (which typically makes them uncomfortable). When I take my kids to the park I am thinking about all the things I need to be getting done. So on and on it goes.

This is a painful confession for me to make, but it is totally true. My children can tell you that in order for me to play with them, they have to coerce me. Sad to say, but their pleas sound something like this:

> "Go under water, Mommy! Get your hair wet! Please, please, please!" My children beg me.
>
> "Yeah! She went under!"
>
> "Wow! Look! Her hair's wet! Can you believe it?"
>
> "Let's play sharks-and-minnows, Mom!"
>
> "Go down the slide with us, Mom! You'll have fun! Play with us!"
>
> "Get your golf clubs, Mom! You can hit some balls with us! Let's go outside and play!"
>
> "Let's play Monopoly, Mom! I'll set it up! All you have to do is play! I'll get it all set up!"
>
> "Let's dance, Mommy. I want to dance. I'll turn on the music and we'll dance together!"
>
> "Let's play hide-and-seek, Mommy. I count and you go hide. One. Two. Three. Four. Five. Six. Seventeen. Nineteen. Twenty. Twenty-one...."
>
> "Let's play restaurant, Mommy. I'll bring you the food. All you have to do is eat!"
>
> "Please play Bible Man, Mommy. You can be the Gossip Queen." (I wonder where they got *that* idea.)

Do you see what I'm saying here? They almost have to *beg* me to cut loose and live a little. I just really don't know how to play. You see, I am one of the Type A personalities who really must work at having a merry heart. I am not a naturally cheerful person. Only weeks ago, I felt very impressed by God that I absolutely must smile more, especially around personalities I find challenging. Cheerfulness and playfulness are not qualities my family is completely devoid of, but they are also not our dominant traits. We are, however, known more for working. Work, work, work! That's what was emphasized most in my family.

Aside from not knowing how to play, much of my excuse for not playing with my kids in the past has just been that I have allowed myself to be weighed down by the cares of life. Too many days with financial concerns. Too many misunderstandings with my spouse. Too many friends going through life-and-death crises. Too many betrayals. Too many hurts. Too many disappointments. Too many changes to adjust to and too many moves. And all the while, my children grow taller, their voices grow deeper, and I've noticed as time goes by, that my older child's desire to play like the little child he once was diminishes. He rarely invites me to play anymore.

"When I get through with this horrible season in my life," I promise myself, "then I'll play with my kids."

"When we get settled finally, then there will be time to laugh."

"When we come out of this financial mess, then I can feel free to play and enjoy life."

"After I get this book finished, then I can lie in the grass and relax."

"When I get through this project, or that...." On and on the excuses go. All the while, my children grow.

What I am beginning to understand is that maintaining a cheerful playful spirit is as much a discipline and spiritual necessity as having the fruits of love and self-control. It is as essential to being a good mother as is knowing how to change a diaper. I myself have to work at playing! I have to schedule it into my life, as necessary as work or sleep! Recreation is vital to a healthy life and attitude. Think of that!

The Bible tells us in Proverbs 17:22 *A merry heart doeth good like a medicine.* A merry heart is one that takes time out to enjoy the moment, to rest and to play. All work and no play won't keep the doctor away. Rather, it will burn you out and wear down your immunity. Laughter and enjoyment are essential to life and good health. Life was meant to be celebrated.

Years ago, when I worked in healthcare public relations, a woman came to speak to our association. She was a humor therapist for cancer patients in the large cancer center in the South. This tiny woman gained a very great reputation for helping the terminally ill recover. Studies have been done to show that immune systems fight harder when a person is more relaxed and has a merry heart.

This woman was one of the funniest little southern women I had ever heard. She had all kinds of funny hats and props and boas which she made everyone wear throughout her presentation. She even taught us several exercises to get us laughing. She described to us how a strong healthy immune system was so closely tied to the ability to laugh and produce endorphins in the body. She was successful in getting us all laughing harder than I had ever laughed before. We laughed and laughed. All of us together—a room full of stuffy, stressed, serious public relations people sitting there wearing funny hats and glasses and masks, laughing like there were no cares in the world. Her primary point was straight from Proverbs: *A merry heart doeth good like a medicine.*

Just when she began to get us all worked up, she started giving us a lesson in biology. She pointed out the location of the thymus gland. "It is this gland which is responsible for producing endorphins to the brain and responds to laughter much in the same way it responds to exercise," she said in her funny entertaining way. "You have to stimulate your thymus on a regular basis. I recommend to all my patients that you *thump* your thymus!" She was dead serious.

"Come on, let's all do it together," I remember her saying as she knocked her fist on the area just below her throat.

About that time I was thinking to myself, *this woman is crazy.* I began looking around the room to see which one made the dumb decision to hire this woman to come and speak. We all began laughing at her and just stared in disbelief at how nutty she looked thumping her thymus.

"I'm not kidding," she shrieked at us. **"Start thumping!"**

Of course, this was all part of the humorous act, but in almost immediate response, we started thumping. And the more we thumped, the more we laughed. We laughed 'til it hurt! All of us. When we finally settled down and were able to stop laughing, I felt like I had been on a three-week vacation at a world class spa. All of a sudden all the cares of my job back at the hospital and all the problems with my budget, negative press reports, demanding administrators and mounds of work I carried into the meeting just melted away! *A merry heart doeth good like a medicine!*

One of my favorite portraits of Jesus is the one known as *The Laughing Jesus.* It's a beautiful portrayal of our Lord with His head back and heartily laughing. I believe Jesus loved life and He loved to laugh even though He knew He was born to die. Jesus died so that we could have a merry heart, an abundant life, and enjoy each day God gives us. I believe Jesus was cheerful and we should be, too! In Romans 12:8 we are told that we should do our service to God with cheerfulness. Strong's defines *cheerfulness* as *serene joyfulness.*

Psalm 37:4 (one of my favorite Scriptures that I display in my home) says, *Delight yourself in the Lord and He will give you the desires of your heart.* Delight! Think of that! That's all He wants us to do—rest in Him and delight. That word *delight* means *to take great pleasure in something.*

Now, let's take that and apply it to our children. If we as mothers can teach our children the practice of cheerfulness, and if we can teach them to take great pleasure in God, even when the going gets rough, then we have given them an important key to victorious living. When God Himself becomes our total heart's desire, and when we learn to just delight in His presence, our lives become a beautiful portrait of love for the world to see. The joy of the Lord will be our strength (See Nehemiah 8:10).

I once attended a Bible study which was led by a wonderful woman of God who taught on cheerfulness. Ending our sessions for the summer vacation, she presented each of us with a small gift and reminder of her teaching that will forever remain in my memory. On a bright yellow 3 x 5 card, she taped a miniature pinwheel. On it was written *A cheerful heart does good like a medicine* (Proverbs 17:22). As we all dispersed for the summer months, she admonished us all to remain *cheerful* in our homes and teach our children to be the same. The pinwheel card was for us to display on a desk or in our kitchen as a reminder that when challenges arise, stay positive and cheerful.

"I chose a pinwheel," she said as she blew on it, "because they remind us to be playful, happy and carefree." I still have that little card and pinwheel. It has seen me through some not so cheerful circumstances and days. But the lesson I learned that day was that cheerfulness is a choice. Having a merry heart is a choice. Playfulness with our children is a choice. Do you choose to be cheerful when there is no money? When things aren't going well with your spouse? When there is no spouse? When there's illness?

I have watched and learned from my dear friends who have battled cancer and illness. While through it all, they have remained some of the most positive and cheerful people I know. I have learned from some of my girlfriends whose spouses have left them for other women, and yet they have remained cheerful. I have learned the importance of laughter and being lighthearted from another friend. After three frightening days of being in the waiting room following her best friend's surgery to remove cancer, everyone was emotionally drained. It was my friend who helped us laugh again. She has the gift of keeping things light, happy and emotionally balanced. She is cheerful, and that's one of the things that makes her the strong leader that she is!

These examples are not acts of phony cheerfulness. Rather, it is the choice of these women to remain calm and positive, able to see the good in extremely negative situations. It is He, Jesus, who makes us glad.

So, what do you choose this day, Mom? Depression? Oppression? Self-pity? Isolation? Anger? Irritability? Negativity? Or do you choose cheerfulness, joy, laughter—pinwheels?

What are some ways you can play more with your children? (Be specific.)

____

____

____

____

____

____

____

On the average, how many minutes a day do you laugh? ______
How many minutes a day do your children laugh? ______
How many minutes do you laugh together? ______

How can you increase your laughter?

____

On a scale of 1 to 10, 10 being the strongest, how do you rate your cheerfulness? ______

What are you planning to do to improve or maintain this?

____

How can you better model this to your children?

____

A Mother's Prayer

Father God, help me to choose to be cheerful. Teach me how to play with my children and interact with them in lighthearted ways that will create beautiful memories for them when they're older. I speak a blessing over my children that they will be cheerful people all the days of their lives and that they will at all times be strengthened by the joy of the Lord. Let our family spread light, laughter, and cheerfulness wherever You send us, Lord. Teach us to laugh and to rest in You.

In Jesus' name I pray. Amen.

CHAPTER 13

THE MARVELOUS MADNESS OF RAISING GRATEFUL CHILDREN

...*Be ye thankful.* Colossians 3:15

"Look up at your teacher and say thank you." My children hear me say it after Sunday school class. In some crazy way I keep reminding them because I have this fear that if I don't, they won't remember to say thank you and we'll all appear to be ungrateful which, of course, is pride. I want people to say, "Your children are the most well-behaved, most respectful children." And people frequently do, but even still, I have this suspicion that they just haven't yet fully grasped the concept of being grateful to those who pour into their lives. Therefore, they need me there to constantly hound them with my usual reminder, "What do you say?"

"Thank you," they reply.

Many times I find myself having to remind them to say thank you for everyday things that you would expect them to remember on their own. Some of you are laughing about now because you know you do the same thing. Now, if I am totally honest with you, maybe part of the reason why they don't totally grasp the concept of saying thank you and being grateful is because I myself have not yet fully grasped it and have not modeled it well enough in my own home. Selah (Pause and think).

The truth is, saying thank you is a fruit of the spirit of gratitude. Notice I said gratitude, not grumbling. Let's get that straight because sometimes I get the two confused. Grumbling and complaining are direct opposites of gratitude. If we are not spending our time in gratitude, chances are we are grumbling. Being grateful is not a natural human...or female...trait. I must confess that I spend a lot of my housecleaning time grumbling through clenched teeth.

What I am learning is that gratitude has to be taught and sown into the hearts and spirits of our children and my complaining is modeling the exact opposite. Gratitude has to be deeply rooted in our hearts before we can demonstrate it. It is an attitude that is learned from usually—you guessed it—the mother.

That's hard for a mom when circumstances are less than perfect, when life gets tough and you are worn out. My grumbling gets especially bad when I am either hungry or tired—kind of like a toddler. If I start getting ill (pronounced *eel* in the South), many times it's because I haven't eaten and/or I need to rest. Those ten-minute power naps can work wonders! Mix hunger, lack of sleep, and raging hormones together with the pressures of life, and all of a sudden we can become Cruella Deville—if you know what I mean. That's when I advance from grumbling to out-of-control wild woman and somebody in the house is calling the prayer line. Don't y'all sit there and look so innocent!

Ladies, that last paragraph is worth its weight in gold! If we could just do the practical things like eating healthy food, resting, getting proper sleep, and exercising, we could become much better wives and mothers and could better remain in an attitude of thankfulness.

The story of Moses at Meribah contains some valuable lessons about the power of gratitude and the danger of complaining. What I discovered in my studies is that there is a progression to complaining which leads us away from gratitude. You see, the story goes something like this:

Moses has led six million Israelites through the wilderness. They wind up at a place called Meribah, which means *a place of despair, quarreling, strife and provocation.* The Israelites are hot, tired and *very* thirsty. There is no water. This is forty years after the incident at Marah where there was no water. (Just as a side note, after living in a literal desert in Phoenix for nearly six years, I can tell you that you don't want to be in a dry hot place without water!) This is Moses' second go-around with millions of thirsty people. By then, the people had had enough and began complaining to Moses.

Interestingly, one of the first things a survivalist will tell you *not* to do if you find yourself in the desert without water is *talk*. In other words, their very complaining made them thirstier, making matters worse. It probably sounded something like this.

"Moses, are you crazy? Why did you bring us out here in this God-forsaken desert? What were you thinking? We want to go home. We're dying of thirst! What about our children?" (You can imagine them all crying in the background.)

I am sure my husband has felt just like Moses at times as I've begged to go back to the good ole South. Now, it's one thing for us moms to suffer, but when it comes to our children, watch out! We tend to get a little riled up. We start complaining and then all sense of gratitude goes out the window.

The people started murmuring, which means kind of under their breath, teeth clenched—fussing, we used to call it in the South. Then that led to out and out complaining. This means they got up the nerve to approach Moses and really let him have an earful. The complaining led to contention and misunderstanding among them all, which really began to make Moses very angry. The Bible says then that anger leads to strife and quarreling, which further opens the door to all manner of evil (See James 3:16). In other words, all hell breaks loose. Do you see the progression, ladies?

It was about then that Moses got so angry and fed up that he directly disobeyed God, and you know the rest of the story. Instead of speaking to the rock as he was told to do, he struck it. In Southern vernacular—*he hit the fool out of that thang cause he was mad as a hornet.*

I can just see all the Israelites standing there in stunned disbelief. "Uh oh!" "Now what have you done, Moses?" as the water gushed out. There they all stood with their fearless leader and man of God who, by their complaining and grumbling had been provoked to sin, costing him entrance into the promised land.

Do we see the cost of complaining, ladies? I say "we" because I need to get this, too. Do we understand the progression of sin it brings into our lives and the lives of others? More times than not, the disagreements and tense moments of fellowship I have with my husband usually trace back to my complaining!

What if things had been different with the Israelites that day in Meribah? What if they would have had their own intimate relationship with God and had spoken directly to Him instead of relying on Moses? What if they chose, rather than complaining, to say to God, "Lord, we don't know why this is happening and why we are without water, but we trust You. We know that You are a loving and kind God and that no good thing will You withhold from those that love You. We know that water is on the way and it won't be one second too late. We know that You see us and that You hear our cries for help and that nothing is too difficult for You! We remember how You saved us from Egypt. We remember how You rescued us at the Red Sea. We thank You, God, for how You made the bitter waters sweet at Marah! And God, with a heart full of gratitude and thanksgiving, we come before You and we know You will do it again!"

How do you think their children's and babies' lives would have been impacted by that kind of response? How do you think it would have affected Moses? Think of it and let's now translate this to our own lives, challenges and tests. Maybe we should say:

"Father God, I don't know why I am going through this trial, but I thank You that You have me in the palm of Your hand. I thank You, God, that You know exactly what we are going through and that You Yourself have been acquainted with sorrow and grief. I thank You that Your Word says in Philippians 4:19 that You will supply all my needs according to Your riches in glory. I thank You that Your arm is not shortened and You are a mighty God. Nothing is too difficult for You. You are my answer and my hiding place! I trust in You to make this situation right and work it for my good. With a heart full of gratitude and thankfulness, I enter into Your presence and I'm going to remain there and rest. In Jesus' name."

Psalm 100:4 says, *Enter into His gates with thanksgiving.* In other words, the entry point into the presence of God, which is the place where all our needs are met, is in being thankful! We can't teach our children how to get into His presence until first we teach them thankfulness.

We've all been around children who have never been taught how to be thankful. Something I have found difficult is how to respond with grace to someone who doesn't say thank you. Ingratitude can seem like a sense of entitlement that says without words—you need to do for me, provide for me, cater to me, entertain me. Put the mirror to my own face; how many times have I myself modeled this ungrateful behavior to God, to my husband (who, by the way, does nice things for me every day), to my parents, and my children, family and friends.

It is important to *demonstrate* our gratitude to those who have blessed our lives. Sometimes we just assume that others know how much we appreciate them. Growing up, thank you notes were mandatory in our home. My mother wouldn't think of not sending someone a thank you note, even for the smallest favor, and she taught us to do the same. That's just her graceful appreciative nature.

Sad to say, I have not been as diligent with thank you notes as I should be. I stand convicted to do better. I want to be more grateful. I want to be more thankful and demonstrate it. Hope you do, too.

Just a simple thank you makes all the difference in the world. I guess that's why I am such a stickler for wanting my children to look the adult in the eye—that one who taught them or helped them or took time with them—and show some heartfelt gratitude.

At the close of this chapter, my youngest son who has been napping beside me as I write, has wet *my* bed. Oh, I'm *so* thankful! Thankful, thankful, thankful! I guess I'll go wash the sheets now! To practice what I've been preaching, let me say, I'm thankful for a washing machine and a bed to sleep on in the first place. I'm especially thankful for his nap so I could write and thankful that if he had to have an accident in our bed, it was on Edward's side! (Oops! I can't believe I said that!)

Colossians 3:15 says, *Be ye thankful.* What are you thankful for today, moms? Who is it that you need to tell you love and appreciate them? Who is it that you are grateful for? What do you need to thank God for that He has done?

Write the names of those you need to express some gratitude to. You never know how it can help them. Like old Moses, they might be ready to strike the rock.

____

____

____

____

____

Count your blessings and give thanks to God. Name them one by one. Fill in as many as you possibly can.

____

____

____

____

____

____

____

____

A Mother's Prayer

Father God, we enter into Your gates with thanksgiving and into Your courts with praise. We thank You, God, for Your love and Your many blessings. Thank You, God, for our children and family. Thank You, God, for our spouses. Thank You, God, that You are working in all of our lives and that You are making us into a people with a grateful heart.

We repent for the times that we have grumbled and complained, keeping us out of our promised land. We ask You to cleanse every grumbling word by the blood of Jesus and wipe them from Your book. We ask that You fill our mouths and the mouths of our children with praise and thanksgiving that we would be examples of Christ for all to follow.

Help us to always remember to give You thanksgiving, praise and honor for all You have done in our lives, especially when times are hard. And help us to remember to thank those You have sent to bless our lives. I speak a blessing over my children that they will be a grateful and thankful person and that they will teach this to others all the days of their lives.

In Jesus' name I pray. Amen.

CHAPTER 14

THE MARVELOUS MADNESS OF PRAYING OVER YOUR CHILDREN

Praise be to the Lord, my Rock, who trains my hands for war, my fingers for battle. Psalm 144:1

"Ohhhhh…kaaaay! Git out! He's coming!" I could hear my mother and Aunt Sukey yelling in sing-song unison as my siblings, cousins and I would splash around in our grandfather's pond. It was hot in South Georgia in the summertime and there weren't many swimming pools around. If we wanted to take a dip, it had to be in a river, branch or a pond. This afternoon as we had done many times before, we begged to swim with the alligator in Dug Pond. My grandfather named the pond Dug because—you know—he dug it out! I don't know if the alligator had a name or not.

After filling the pond with water, he put some fish in it and a little "pet" alligator. On occasion, our parents and grandparents would take us all there to swim. They would sit in lawn chairs on the bank of one side of the pond where the alligator was and tell us to go swim on the other side. We'd have at least a good thirty minutes or so before that ole alligator saw our splashing around and got curious. Pretty soon, we'd see his little head and eyes on the top of the water, and then here he'd come. We could gauge how fast he was coming by his tail swishing back and forth. As he began to get about a third of the way across the pond, our parents would start yelling. We'd all shriek and laugh and make a big ado about getting out of the water, and then we'd run as fast as we could to the other side. There we'd be safe to swim until the little gator would decide to come back and investigate what we were up to. We'd then have to repeat the process all over again. The things a kid will do for a swim! (Honest to goodness, true story!)

I think my grandfather eventually had to kill that alligator because he got too big eating up all his fish; never mind the danger to his grandchildren! I don't know for sure, but maybe my grandmother served him for supper one night. I'm told they taste like chicken.

"I've never heard of such," you're probably saying. Well, some people have pet bulldogs and some have pet alligators. Therein lies the century-long fight between Georgia Bulldogs and Florida Gators! Incidentally, Dug Pond was near the Georgia-Florida state line.

Hey, I know it's crazy, and I probably would never let my children swim with an alligator! But maybe somehow I can gain some spiritual life lessons from the experience and be better off for it. Besides that, swimming in my granddaddy's pond was just plain old fun. That's kind of like human nature in life. We get into sin because at first it's plain old fun. But the payoff (the wages), I've learned, is death (See Romans 6:23).

If I had to extract a spiritual lesson for mothers from swimming with the alligator, it would be tied to my own little mother who sat beside that pond and never took her eyes off me. At least, she hoped she didn't. She did this all the while knowing right where that little alligator was, as she and my aunt kept watch for danger. They knew when it was getting even remotely close. And they sounded an alarm when trouble was nearing.

Get the point here? As a mother, covering our children in prayer is probably our most important task. We are to sit by the pond, so to speak, and be watch-women over the children. We have been given the spiritual authority and responsibility to cover, watch over, and protect our children from the onslaught of the enemy. It's our job as parents to be a spiritual covering and to recognize when the enemy is trying to get a foothold in our children's lives.

We know and are aware that there is an enemy who is opposed to those who have committed their hearts to Christ. His goal, as described in John 10:10 is to steal, kill and destroy. But Christ has come so that we might have life and life more abundantly.

Paul states that we wrestle (that means close combat) not against flesh and blood. In other words, we're not fighting people. We wrestle against powers, principalities, rulers of darkness, spiritual wickedness in high places (See Ephesians 6:12). That Scripture is evidence that there is a war going on and the enemy continues to fight like he has no clue he has already lost.

Our job is to resist the devil because Christ already won the battle on the cross. James 4:7 tells us to resist the devil and he will flee from you. That word *resist* means *to stand against or protest.* I once heard a powerful sermon about Martin Luther, the father of the Protestant movement. I had never considered it before, but as was pointed out, we call ourselves protestant because we protest. We stand against the work of the devil and protest it. Most importantly, we protest or resist the work of the devil in our children's lives.

Sometimes protesting means that we open our mouths to speak against the evil and injustice around us. Much of the evil we deal with today could have been avoided if we as women of God would have opened our mouths and protested. If we don't do it, mothers, who will? We need a spiritual radar of sorts, known as discernment, which alerts us to pray and to cancel the plans of the enemy in the lives of our children through prayer. We need boldness to speak up when it's time to protest the devil.

For more than thirty years my dear mother and daddy had set this example for our family. Every day, every day, every day…they agree together in prayer and place a covering over all their children and grandchildren. Calling out our names and addresses, they ask for the blood of Jesus to be over our homes, for angels to stand guard around the property, and for us to wear the armor of God which Paul mentions in Ephesians, the sixth chapter. They agree together for our prosperity and our health and for God to open and close the right doors in our lives. They declare blessings and God's goodness over us each day.

When a parent prays for their child, it is always a powerful thing and God listens! The power of the prayer of parents is illustrated so beautifully in the new children's book, *Salt in His Shoes,* written by Mrs. Deloris Jordan about her son Michael Jordan's dream to play basketball. Along with her daughter Roslyn, they recount the desire of Michael as a young boy to grow tall and one day be a basketball legend. The illustrator, Kadir Nelson, included in the story a beautiful picture of Mrs. Jordan kneeling by her bed in prayer. "Dear God, please help Michael to be the best he can be and to give his best in all that he does. And Lord, could You please make him just a little taller tomorrow than he is today? Thank You. Amen."[1] This picture and prayer is my favorite part of the book because it reminds us of the greatness that can come when a mother kneels to pray for her child as she did.

---

1. Deloris Jordan, Roslyn M. Jordan, Kadir Nelson, *Salt in His Shoes: Michael Jordan in Pursuit of a Dream* (New York, NY: Simon & Schuster Children's Publishing, 2003).

I am forever grateful for the thousands of prayers of my mother and dad, and pray that my life will yield the fruit of their spiritual labor for me. But even with that confidence and knowing that someone somewhere is praying for me, it's still my job as a mother to make a stand against the enemy myself! I've got to put the armor of God on myself and my children. And my children have to learn to do the same so they can teach their children.

For nearly eighteen years, Edward and I have prayed together every day. For those first two years of marriage, we didn't understand the importance of it. But for these last eighteen, through thick and thin we've agreed for God's forgiveness, mercy, grace, wisdom, guidance, provision and protection. I believe it is that daily prayer that has kept us together when things got tough.

Several years ago, God gave me a simple way to encourage and teach our children to pray. I like to call this the "wash, dress, go" prayer method. That's simple enough for a child or adult to learn. Just like we have to wash, dress and go each day in the natural, it's necessary to do this for the spirit man as well. If we don't take a bath every day, guess what? We smell. The same is true with our inner man. Thank God for the washing of the water of the Word of God (Eph. 5:26) and for the blood of Jesus which cleanses us from all sin. Thanks be to God that we can go to Him and ask for His forgiveness and to cleanse us from all iniquity and sin as Jesus taught us in the Lord's prayer.

When we come before God in repentance and teach our children to do the same, it's just like taking a wonderful shower that refreshes and cleanses the mind. Part of washing the negativity out of our minds comes from thankfulness. Spending the better part of our prayer just thanking God for all He has done for us helps us to focus on the wonderful blessings of life.

Next we teach our children to make use of the spiritual garments mentioned in the Bible, putting them on. We wouldn't think of letting our children go out the door to school naked! In the same way, we need to make sure they're not spiritually streaking! We are told in 1 Peter 5:8 that Satan roams about like a roaring lion, seeking whom he may devour. He's like the alligator in my granddaddy's pond, just looking for fish food—or in my case, a grandchild to eat. If our children aren't spiritually dressed, they are vulnerable to that attack.

When my mother and I recently discussed Samuel, the prophet in the Bible, we talked about how he was taken to the temple by his mother, Hannah, to be reared by the priests. Samuel was the long awaited son Hannah thought she would never have. She made a deal with God and vowed that if He would give her a son, she would dedicate him back. Releasing little Samuel to the care of priests many miles away from her home for the rest of his life must have been excruciating. I am sending my third grader away to a week of church camp in the morning, and I feel like I might back out! Hannah, nonetheless, was true to her promise to God.

But the one thing my mother so aptly pointed out that I had never considered was that each year when Hannah was allowed to visit Samuel at the temple, she brought him a new coat. This wasn't just any coat, but a special coat that she had handmade. Each year, as Samuel grew, Hannah had to make a little larger coat. What the Holy Spirit showed my mother in that story was that the coat Hannah made was like a spiritual covering that she put on her beloved son. As he got older, he needed even more covering.

The same is true with our children today and I guess that's why my mother prays harder for me now than she did when I was swimming with an alligator. We as mothers must place that covering over our children. I hear some of you asking as you read this, "So how do we cover our children and grandchildren?" Paul said to put on the *whole* (that means all of it) armor of God that you may be able successfully to stand up against (all) the strategies and the deceits of the devil (See Eph. 6:11).

Let's look briefly at the pieces of the armor. First, Paul mentions the helmet of salvation to put on our head. This protects our minds and thought life. It keeps our minds girded up with the salvation of Christ. Then we put on the breastplate of righteousness which protects the heart and the breath of the spirit man within us. Another piece is the girdle or belt of truth. This belt goes around the center of our spirit man to keep our lives balanced in truth. Lies and deception open the door to the enemy. Without truth, we have allowed open access to the devil to come in and bring destruction. On the feet, we are told to put on the shoes of the preparation of the gospel of peace. Jesus said in Luke 10:19 that He has given us power to tread on serpents, scorpions, and over all the power of the enemy and nothing by any means shall hurt us. Put your shoes on!

The shield of faith we hold up to repel and protect us from all the fiery darts of the enemy. Anything he tries to send our way, we deflect with our shield of faith! Next is the sword of the Spirit which is the Word of God. Hebrews 4:12 makes reference to the Word being sharper than any two-edged sword. With sharp edges on both sides, you can hit the enemy one way and then come back with the other side.

Lastly, Paul says to remember to pray in the spirit always. Praying in the spirit is part of the wardrobe and arsenal we have to resist the enemy. The Bible also talks about the importance of putting on love, humbling ourselves, putting on the robe of righteousness, and putting on the garment of praise for the spirit of heaviness. If we didn't need garments for our spiritual man, why would God have included them in the Word? And if we weren't in a war, why would God have given us armor?

After we learn to wash in the water of the Word and dress in the armor, next we must *go*! Go out and serve Christ with all our hearts. Go out and win the lost. Don't keep the blessings of God all bottled up inside. Share it wherever you go. We used to sing a little children's song to the tune of "Go Tell It on the Mountain" that went something like this: *Go tell it on the playground, down the slide and on the swing. Go tell it on the playground that Jesus Christ is born!* Children can go, too, knowing that their lives can make a difference for the kingdom of God.

Trust that your steps are ordered of the Lord and He will go before you to open the doors that no man can close, and close the doors that no man can open. Revelation 3:7 tells us that God will use us in astounding ways when we pray and ask Him to!

I hear you asking, "So you mean you say all that out loud?" You bet I do! Just thanking God out loud is releasing a powerful force. Romans 10:10 says that confession is made unto salvation. That Scripture is referring to the salvation of our eternal souls, but can also apply to the importance of confessing the Word on a daily basis. We are saved from the onslaught of the enemy when we open our mouth, using the Word of God.

A visual example I could give you is about an old stray dog that would come up on the farm. My grandmother would walk out there, put her hands authoritatively on her hips, and yell, "Now, git!" That stray dog would tuck his tail every time and run away as fast as he could. That's a good picture of the enemy when we rebuke him using the powerful name of Jesus and make a confession of the Word.

Ladies, we need to learn to man our post in prayer over our children, our husbands, our homes and our lives. There have been some seasons in my life that I had been slack on this, and there was a price to pay. Just like my little mother wouldn't think of leaving her post by that pond as I swam with the alligator, I'm not going to leave my spiritual post and shirk my responsibilities to cover my family in prayer.

Let's pray that we teach our children to do it, too! They may not always pray now with my prompting, but one day, as I did, they'll recognize they've got to do it themselves. Girls, whether you know it or not, there are alligators in the pond! Let's wake up, man our post, and sound the alarm!

How do you cover your children in prayer?

____

____

____

____

____

____

____

What are some of the specific things God has shown you to pray for your children?

____

____

____

____

____

____

____

A Mother's Prayer

Father God, this is the time for me to wake up. This is the time to sound the alarm. This is the time for me to shake myself out of a spiritual stupor and resist the enemy. This is the time that I will faithfully each day pray a prayer covering over my home, my marriage, my children. This is the time that I will speak a blessing over our lives and our future. This is the time that I will put on the armor of God and pray without ceasing.

God, help me to be like the watchman on the wall for my family and to exercise the gift of discernment in all matters. Help me to remember each day as I have just read to WASH, DRESS, and GO. I plead the blood of Jesus over my spouse, my children, and myself. I put all the pieces of the armor on each of us. (Name each piece.) I ask for angels to be released on our behalf to accompany us wherever we go and to keep us out of harm's way.

I thank You that the steps of a righteous man and woman are ordered of the Lord. We are the righteousness of God in Christ Jesus and wear the robe of righteousness around us. I speak a blessing over my children and grandchildren that they will be prayer warriors and that You will train their hands to war against the enemy. Thank You, God, that You have caused us to tread on serpents, scorpions, and over all the power of the enemy and that nothing by any means will harm us. Thank You, God, that You have made us more than conquerors through Christ our Lord and Savior. Amen.

CHAPTER 15

THE MARVELOUS MADNESS OF MARITAL RELATIONS

(What Your Mama Never Told You About Sex & Motherhood)

Let thy fountain be blessed, and rejoice with the wife of your youth. Proverbs 5:18

Well, girls, let's all take a deep breath as we delve into a chapter that originally I had no intention of writing. After some prayer and contemplation I feel it is, oh, so vital to the success of motherhood. One of the important areas of being a good mother is being a good wife. In order to be a good wife and to have a happy, healthy marriage, you need a happy healthy sex life. Just ask your husband.

It's a subject that for the most part a "sweet" but slightly prudish girl like myself would never want to discuss for the sheer horror of thinking about my mother, pastors, friends and family reading it. I am not as worried about my dad because, after forty years of medicine, he has just about seen and heard it all.

I can tell you this. If you are not satisfied in this area, and more importantly, not satisfying your husband, somebody's going to be cranky. I was remembering the other day what it was like when the OB/Gyn gave us clearance to have—well, you know—after the birth of our first child. This kind of thing is really important to a new dad and pretty much a non-issue to most new moms. Dads may not tell you how important this is to them, but it is!

Our first child, Davis, was one of those babies you could rarely put down without him screaming. Because he slept in a bassinet in our room for the first few months, my husband and I found it difficult to resume—well, you know. Anyway, there was this one little musical ducky toy that Davis loved and when you put it into the bassinet and wound it up, you would have at least two minutes of peace at a time. The music went to the tune of *The Blue Danube* by Johann Strauss. *Dun, dun, dun, dun, dun—quack quack, quack quack. Dun, dun, dun, dun, dun—quack quack, quack quack.* You know the song.

Being a mom with a premature baby, I was too afraid to put him in another room for—well, you know—fifteen minutes or so, to give my starved husband some attention. I got this bright idea that we'd just put Davis in the bassinet in a far corner of the room, crank up the old ducky and see how far we got. (If you were here with me now, I'd give you a wink.)

So there we went, girls, to the sounds of the quacker, trying to rekindle the hot, steamy fire and passion we once knew for seven years before this five-pound person came into our lives. Every time the music would stop, the baby would scream and one of us would have to get up, go over and wind up the ducky. I don't know how many times we had to repeat that process just to achieve "success." With a twenty-eight day hospital stay, almost two and a half months had gone by since we had been together. There wasn't any ducky going to stop us!

There began my experience with sex as a mother! There…I said it. Do you feel better? Hopefully we've learned a few things since that first night over twelve years ago. So, my husband and I decided together to come up with a brief list for all you couples out there about—well, you know—with children in the house! Here goes. Men, you're going to love this.

1. Set the mental mood.

My husband and I have a system of communication that lets one another know "tonight's the night." (I bet you can just guess who gives the most signals.) Some friends of ours back in Georgia used to have a standing appointment on Saturday night. On Saturdays, he would begin teasing and hinting that he desired to have sex. He would look at her with the biggest smile sometime during the day and say, "It's Saturday night!" We would all laugh so hard. It was so funny back then. But the older I get, the more I realize, maybe it's not so funny.

Part of setting the mood for romance is to express a desire to be together. In the book *For Women Only*[1], the survey of men showed that one of the most important things to husbands *concerning* sex was that their *wives* showed a desire for *them*. The survey also showed that unanimously, men agreed that sex was fundamental to their overall well being and ability to succeed in life. Interesting, possibly because our men see our desire as mothers to constantly dote and care for our children, they somehow feel neglected.

One of my friends transparently shared how every night—yes, every night—she gives her husband a massage and prays over him so he can rest better. She went on to say that if anything happened to her, she never wanted him to feel that she didn't touch him enough. Now, that's love, girls.

I hear you asking, "So what do I do if I don't desire to have sex with my husband?" Maybe too many sleepless nights with a baby, too many soccer games, too many late nights waiting up on a teenager to come home, too many long days at work, too many extra pounds, or too much selfishness have caused your desire to wane. "Yes, that's me. What should I do?"

---

1. Shaunti Feldhahn, *For Women Only: What You Need to Know about the Inner Lives of Men* (Sisters: Multnomah Publishers Inc., 2004).

Girlfriends, I hear your pleas and cries. I'm with you, baby! It's hard to feel very sexy with ten loads of laundry on the floor, a sink full of dirty dishes and you're dead tired. I know. And here's the conclusion I have come to: If you feel you aren't able to demonstrate your desire to your husband—are you ready for this—if you will give unselfishly to your husband, the desire does come!

Just make the decision that you and your husband are going to have a fulfilling sex life together. Choose to give your spouse the love and attention they desire and long for. What I have found is that desire and healing of a relationship often follow our unselfishness and willingness to be intimate with our spouse.

Take off that "mommy hat" for the night. Light a candle. Put on some romantic tunes. Brush your hair. Put on some lipstick. Slap on some progesterone cream! Remove those nursing pads! Put on some high heels. Eat your Wheaties! Come on, girl! You can do it! You'll be glad you did!

2. Set the atmosphere.

Somehow, a stuffed Barney doll just doesn't do much for intimacy in the bedroom. Neither do Legos and army men under the sheets, which can actually be quite uncomfortable! Smelly diapers, breast pumps, children's tennis shoes and dirty socks really don't add much to the ambience either. You see, after a while a mother will agree that we become immune to the fact that these items are killing the romance in our life.

Think about the atmosphere. What does it speak about your desire to be with your husband? A clean comfortable room with nice clean sheets does wonders for the experience. As a mother caring for kids all the time, anything we can do to make our time with our husbands more exciting and enjoyable is good. When it comes to expressions of desire, most men appreciate even the smallest efforts like candles, music, massage oil, a warm bath, and words of admiration and love.

In addition to making our physical setting more appealing, our men desperately need our spoken words of affirmation and praise on a regular basis. Part of setting the atmosphere of intimacy is to express those. After cheering, encouraging and affirming kids all day, sometimes the last thing I want to do at night is blubber all over my husband.

At a low point in our marriage, Edward and I had gone for some counseling. The primary counsel to me at that time was that I needed to be Edward's number one cheerleader. I needed to say encouraging and affirming words to him. Things had gotten so bad between us at that point that I literally sat across from his desk with pen and paper in hand and said, "Can you give me some ideas?"

Let me tell you, girls; that counsel was right! Flattering someone is a counterfeit of true admiration. When the wayward woman lured in the young man in Proverbs 7:5, she did it by flattery. The young man void of understanding bought it hook, line and sinker. For this reason, our husbands need to hear those words from us. If we don't say words of admiration and praise to our husbands, some other chick-a-dee will! And I better not hear you saying, "Well, who would want him?" Think about it; you did!

Now back to setting an intimate atmosphere. I once heard the good advice to make your bedroom like a retreat and your bathroom like a mini-spa. The Song of Solomon makes many references to perfuming your bed and linens with myrrh and other spices. In our fast-paced modern day, we'd do well to remove home offices, bills, computers and televisions from the bedroom. This does a lot for you relationship, and helps you get better rest as well.

Just to give you the visual, at this moment I would have to say to myself, "Becky, take down the ironing board! Put away the vacuum cleaner. Put some sheets on your bed! Pick up those books!" While our bedroom is a long way from achieving the retreat status, for the pleasure of my husband and my marriage, I think making the bed like a retreat is a worthy goal.

Let's kick the office and kids out and reclaim our place of intimacy and rest. Close the door and lock it after everyone's asleep and enjoy some private time together. Oh, I'm blushing now! Excuse me for a moment, ladies. I feel like tidying up my bedroom.

3. Be quiet and discreet.

The book of Proverbs talks a lot about discretion. Proverbs 2:11 says that discretion shall preserve you. Children do not need exposure to or ideas of your private time alone with your husband. First of all, it is none of their business, and secondly, to use their own terminology, it would gross them out!

The other day while putting away some towels in my son's bathroom, I was mortified to clearly hear the conversation of my children who were down the hallway in our bedroom! *Oops,* I thought. *If I can hear them this well, I wonder what noises have been piping through the vents for my son to hear at night?* How embarrassing! In a house with teenagers or pre-teens, you can never assume that everyone is asleep, if you know what I mean.

Maybe if we and our husbands really need some "intense" privacy, we should invest in a weekend away somewhere. Talk about needing some intense privacy! As I'm writing just now, I am interrupted by a blood curdling scream after my youngest son shot my oldest son's friend in the head with an air soft gun at close range. Get the ice; check for blood; call the mom?

Okay, I'm back. Minimal damage; the child is fine. "No more guns in the house," I am barking. Where was I? Oh yes, the need to get away....

Most marriage experts agree that every couple needs to have at least a weekend away from the children every so often. Edward and I went much too long—probably a year—before spending a weekend in a hotel alone after our third child. It felt like we hadn't been alone in forever, and quite frankly, I didn't know how to act! I was even a little scared, so much so that I remember staying in the bathroom and plucking my eyebrows for nearly an hour after we got there. Edward was beginning to think I had passed out or something.

Finally after a while I sheepishly emerged from the bathroom to find my husband patiently waiting. It had been so long since we had been alone with no children to interrupt every sentence, I felt like I needed to go over, shake hands and introduce myself. You know what I'm saying? If you can arrange a night away, just the two of you, it does wonders for your marriage.

Discretion with children protects them from any dramatic revelations before they are ready. I mean, do you really want your eight-year-old coming in the next day and finding your sexy nighty?

"Awooo, Mom, what's this?" I can hear them asking. Let's not kid ourselves, moms. Children are exposed to so much now that their minds already are beginning to work overtime in the area of sex, especially boys. Testosterone flows freely at our house! Being discreet (not prudish) with them about your relationship is a way to protect your children's own thought life.

One time a young couple, very passionate toward one another, sat in front of us in church. Well, they started, shall I say, "loving" on one another with a great open show of affection, right there in the middle of service. Things got so heated up that a few of us were fanning ourselves with the bulletin. Several single young men sitting directly behind then, in a desire to keep their thoughts pure, had to get up and move. And this was all before the offertory! My oldest son leaned over and whispered, "Mom, they need to get a room." From the mouth of babes! Discretion; do you see what I'm saying?

4. And finally, run—don't walk!

This is our fourth and final bit of advice, and this one comes from my husband. When the sitter or a friend comes to take your children for a movie or a hamburger, and for just a brief moment you and your husband have the house to yourselves...RUN, don't WALK!

Run like a pair of wild rabbits! Run to your bedroom or wherever you need to "meet up" to experience some intimacy with your spouse. Just try not to knock one another down in the process. I mean, when it comes to having some time alone with your honey in your house, you may have to be a little rude about it! I almost thought I heard Edward yell to our friend and our children as they were leaving, "Don't let the door hit you on your way out!" (Of course, I am kidding here!)

When presented with the opportunity to have the house to yourselves, recognize and relish the moment! Hmmm, maybe that's why my friends who've just sent their last child off to college always have big smiles on their faces. Come to think of it, maybe that's why grandparents are so happy, too!

Those of us with younger children and teens can only dream of the day. So, as soon as the sitter arrives for the "outing" and you've waved goodbye to the little darlings, as in Monopoly, *Do not pass go; do not collect two hundred dollars!* In other words, don't answer the phone and don't open the mail. Don't discuss your child's orthodontist appointment or the D on their math test. Don't stop to pet the dog or water the plants. Don't even stop to "retreat-ize" your bedroom! Just go with the moment! You can't waste this precious time. Your marriage and your motherhood may very well depend on it!

Enjoy that man God has given you! Treasure him. This may sound a bit old fashioned, but women, make sure he is satisfied. When he's satisfied, you are, too. Sexual intimacy with your husband helps take some of the madness *out* of motherhood. When I go over the edge, start grabbing my hair at the scalp and yelling at my kids, "You're driving me crazy," that's when I know I am overdue for some...well, you know. That's when I need to call someone and say, "Please, will you come over and get these kids—now!"

Well, fellow moms, this chapter is almost finished and I hope that something here has inspired you to enjoy your husband a little more. I can tell you this: After nearly twenty years of marriage, we've still "got it." We still have a passion and desire for one another and we're just getting started! Ooo-la-la!

(That wasn't too painful, was it?)

List some things you deeply love and admire about your husband.

____

____

____

____

____

Now go and tell him…Go on!

Write some things you can do to make your bedroom more romantic and enjoyable. (Small things, girls, not to include ripping out walls or buying thousands of dollars worth of new furniture! You know how we can be!)

____

____

Write some specific things you plan to do to express more desire for your husband (or future husband).

A Mother's Prayer

Father God, thank You for the beauty of oneness and the covenant relationship You have given my husband and me to enjoy together. Thank You that out of our love and oneness, You have blessed us with precious children. Help us to always put You first and in the center of our relationship and to unselfishly give to one another. We speak a blessing over our union together that it would be forever filled with Your love and Your presence.

In Jesus' name I pray. Amen.

CHAPTER 16

THE MARVELOUS MADNESS OF MOVING WITH CHILDREN

Neither shall ye build house, nor sow seed, nor plant vineyard, nor have any. But all your days ye shall dwell in tents; that ye may live many days in the land where ye be strangers. Jeremiah 35:7

Something intrigues me about the Rechabites. They were a tribe of people mentioned in the thirty-fifth chapter of Jeremiah, who were devoted to God and who had made a vow to their father, Jonadab. Now Jonadab was a great-nephew of King David and was a man who deeply opposed idolatry. In loyalty to their father Jonadab, the Rechabites promised to live a simple life, to drink no wine, and to live in tents all their days.

Just the other day, as I was packing boxes for my third move in a few years, I was complaining to God about how much I hated this whole process. I was going on and on about how in every move I was the only one in the family who packed the boxes. I murmured to myself about how every box that had ever been packed in our family's history, or ever would be packed, would have to be packed by me. I carried on and on as my husband and sons tried to enjoy the exhilarating end of the golf tournament on TV.

About then I graduated to ranting that they better not expect me to prepare dinner since I was the one doing all the work. Not getting the reaction I had hoped for, I then opted for pity, choking back sobs of how difficult this all was for me and how bad my back was hurting. My husband and children still seemed to be unimpressed by all my drama!

It was about then I felt "directed" by the Holy Spirit to take a break from my labor and tantrum to be led to the thirty-fifth chapter of Jeremiah. There I sat on the couch, completely convicted of my sin through the story of the Rechabites. As I began this reading, I was feeling pretty justified in my complaint to God about another move. But then all of a sudden, out jumped the words from the page of the Bible, "Ye shall dwell in tents."

Dwell in tents, Lord? I thought to myself. *You've got to be kidding me! That means those people moved around a lot.* I guess dwelling in tents meant that they and their families couldn't really settle or get too used to one place. I guess living in a tent meant that they didn't have stainless steel appliances, granite countertops or travertine floors, either. I suppose they didn't have the latest front-loading washer and dryer. They didn't have a home of their own.

"What did they have?" I sensed the Holy Spirit questioning. I sat there a moment and read and reread that sentence, *They dwelt in tents.* I had to think about it a moment and then the answer hit me. They had much! They were rich! They were blessed! They were blessed in loyalty to God, blessed in consecration to God. And here's the lesson God really wanted me to see: they were blessed in mobility. They were rich in the fact that when God said to move, they were willing and able.

Now, I am not suggesting that we all live in tents or move every few years in order to demonstrate mobility! No way. I believe God wants us to prosper and be blessed with wonderful homes and happy memories. It just so happened that career changes and circumstances out of my control prompted our necessary moves. And I can tell you quite honestly that none of the moves have been fun or easy, whether it was across the country or across the street.

I've never gotten used to moving, especially with children. When financial struggles prompted us to sell our home that I had poured so much of myself into decorating and move into a smaller rental, I was so broken. In those final moments in my home, as the moving truck drove away, I stood alone in the kitchen and said to God, "Well, I did my best." And in that short prayer I was essentially saying in my heart, *I have done my best to make this a home for my family and a place of happy memories. And I will continue to do my best. I will be pliable in Your hands in a difficult situation and believe that You have a plan.*

I have prayed and spoken so many times the promises in the Bible that we would possess good land and that we would own houses we didn't build and vineyards we didn't plant. I believe those promises are true. But I also believe this: that if God says move, like the Rechabites, we better be ready, even with children. If God says be mobile, we must be willing.

You see, what God was trying to communicate to me that day was that mobility and flexibility are attitudes of the heart that I must demonstrate in my Christian walk. A willing heart says, "God, wherever You lead me, I will follow." When time is up here, and God seems to be closing a door, we have to go. Moving can sometimes be difficult and sad. But when we go in the power of the Holy Spirit and led by Him, He will build a bridge from the place we are in to the place He is moving us.

Shortly after our move from my beloved home state of Georgia to Phoenix, I was in a local department store. As I rode the elevator to the second floor, I began to hear the piano music playing the song, "Georgia on My Mind." "Not that song," I spoke out loud to God. "I can't take that song."

"Georgia, Georgia. No peace I find. Like an old sweet song keeps Georgia on my mind," the song continued. Pretty soon I found myself getting teary-eyed and singing along with the piano. Silly, I know. What happened next I now recognize as the leading of the Holy Spirit.

As I made my way over to the gift department, my eyes were immediately fixed on a little pillow with the beautiful embroidered words, "Grow where you are planted," Picking it up, as the final chorus of that familiar sentimental song was being played, I decided to buy the pillow. It was a spontaneous purchase that I hadn't intended to make, but nonetheless, one of the most important ones I have ever made. That pillow has been displayed in my room for these past ten years in Phoenix, a constant reminder that *God, You have me here. And while I am here, I'm going to grow! I'm going to blossom. I am going to serve You with my whole heart. I am going to make wonderful friends and memories. I am going to live and enjoy. And more importantly, so are my children.*

As most of you can attest, moving with children is much different than moving without them. From a practical standpoint, children create a lot more packing and preparation. I won't address those aspects here. And I won't discuss the marvelous madness of moving all those toys, clothes, shoes, books, school projects, sports paraphernalia, and other items. And I won't spend a lot of time talking about the mounds of food, trash, cups, toys and dust under my children's beds and sofas where they've stashed them. Having just moved, that's all too fresh for me.

What I do want to encourage in this chapter, is to consider your move from your child's point of view. Think about their feelings. Think about the changes they incur as a result and pray about ways you as a mother can take some of the madness out of the move for your children. Think about their experience as the "new kid" on the block. Consider the challenges they will face in a new school or environment. Think about their feelings in giving up their old bedroom and sleeping somewhere new. Yes, I think we all agree that kids adapt and are quite resilient. However, sometimes they may need a little prayer and preparation to ensure a smooth and happy transition.

I remember the first night in our home after a move. Hamilton was so upset his teeth were chattering as he lay in bed trying to go to sleep. We had prayed with him, but he was still struggling with leaving his old room. About that time, our friend and music pastor knocked at the door as Edward and I continued to unpack. We asked him, "Would you please go in and pray for Hamilton. He's really having a hard time with this move."

Pastor did pray for Hamilton that night and he was able to finally drift off to sleep in peace. It had never occurred to me before then to consider how much a move affects our children and how much they need our prayer to transition. Prior to that night, I always had the insensitive attitude, "Well, we're moving, kids; get over it." Thank God for pastors sent into our lives!

In a recent time of devotion with my children, I felt led to read the story of the rich young ruler in Matthew nineteen. This young man had a desire to please Jesus and wanted Him to know he was faithful to follow the commandments. Jesus, however, was not quite impressed by all this boasting and responded to the man with three important directives. First, he was to sell everything he owned. Second, he was to give all the money to the poor. And thirdly, Jesus said to follow Him.

After reading this story to my children, they were staring at me wide-eyed and I could see I had their attention. So I asked the question, "How do you feel about that?" My middle son responded first by saying he was afraid that now the rich young ruler wouldn't have a home or anything in it.

"He'll be poor," Hamilton said.

"No, he won't!" My oldest son, Davis, refuted. "He would be blessed now with more because he gave it to God."

Then I knew that they were really grabbed by the story and wanted to see what the young ruler decided to do. We continued reading to "discover" that the rich young ruler walked away sadly because he didn't want to sell his home and give it all to the poor. He suffered from a deficiency of understanding and being able to see how little he really had when compared to the heavenly treasures he would have received.

I translated that story in "kid" language to say, "If God tells us to give something up and follow Him somewhere else, what should we do?"

"Sell it all and give it to the poor," Hamilton said. The other two agreed.

Now, I don't know if I'm ready to sell it **all** and give it away. I like some of my stuff; you know what I'm saying. Maybe this young man felt the same way. God is still working on me. But I can tell you that one thing He is trying to get through to me in our recent moves is to remain flexible and mobile, like the Rechabites. That's more important than the purchase of packing tape and boxes. More essential than moving men and realtors is the spiritual preparation, prayer and resolve of heart that no matter where He leads me, I will follow.

Once we make that a priority as mothers, the rest is easier. You see, His yoke is easy and His burden is light. When that prayer and preparation cover our move and our children, we can go forward with the confidence that we will grow where we are planted. We *will* as a family prosper and make a difference for Christ where He leads.

How can you communicate to your children that your home here on earth is temporary and heaven is the place of our citizenship?

____

____

____

____

____

What are some specific ways you can prepare your family or others for a move and make it more peaceful? (Example: First, ask God to lead you to the church you are to attend, second....)

____

____

____

____

____

A Mother's Prayer

Father God, help me to remain pliable in Your hands. Help me not to get too attached to any earthly blessing You have given. I want to be willing to follow You wherever You lead. I believe You for a blessed life, a good home and a prosperous future no matter where You may take us, knowing that we will be blessed in the city and blessed in the field. I trust You with my future, my spouse's future and my children's future. I believe that the best is yet to come in our lives. I speak a blessing over my children that they will follow Your leading and guidance all their days and that in Your perfect love they'll find complete contentment and rest.

In Jesus' name I pray. Amen.

CHAPTER 17

THE MARVELOUS MADNESS OF DISCIPLINING YOUR CHILDREN

He openeth also their ear to discipline. Job 36:10

"You're not going to grab me, are you, Mommy?" my three-year-old asked.

"No, honey, I'm not and I'm so sorry I did," I said in shame. "Mommy was wrong and I ask your forgiveness.'

"I forgive you," came the innocent little response.

Saddened by my ungodly show of anger and complete lack of patience, I vowed to never again lash out at him. Convicted of my sin, I never again wanted to disguise it by calling it discipline.

I had had one of those days where the marvelous madness of motherhood had taken me over the edge. The whining, the tantrums, the disobedience, the fighting, all had taken their toll. I had had enough. You know the limit a mother can take. Truett had thrown one tantrum too many, and now it was time for me to throw mine. Are you with me on this, mothers?

Here's the sin. I reached down and grabbed his shirt collar at the neck, jerked him close to my face so I'd be sure to have his attention, and yelled through clenched teeth, "Stop it! Do you hear me?" (I'm sure he could; the neighbors probably could, too.) "I have had enough of your behavior and I won't take it anymore."

"Okay," came the frightened response. "I'll be good." Then it was quiet for the next several minutes. No more whining, no more fighting, no more complaining from this child. Success, but at what price?

Now you know truthfully this was not the first time I had ever lost it with my children. Nor it is, I am sad to say, the worst disciplining mistake I have ever made. I could curl your ears with some of my blunders. I won't even begin to suggest that I have the answers when it comes to disciplining children. It's a subject that continues to make me scratch my head in wonder. It is by far the most difficult aspect of parenting for me.

Far too many great Christian books and teachings are out there for me to presume to know anything. I've tried to read all the books I could and attend as many parenting courses as I could, and they all have great advice and suggestions. But it seems that even with all the knowledge and education, there is a great chasm between the bad behavior of my children and my reaction when my pain and tolerance threshold has reached its max.

The only two valuable pieces of advice I can give anyone about disciplining your children, and I've learned this from mistakes, is to never discipline in anger. When you do, be quick to ask for forgiveness. Notice I didn't say *if* you do; I say *when* you do. Let's face it, girls; even the best of parents struggle with becoming angry with their children from time to time. It's then that the "ignite" button has been pushed and you are ready to go into orbit if that precious baby does one more thing.

What I am trying to learn is that when that "ignite" button has been pushed, that's the time a little geographical boundary would be in order. In other words, send them to their room or a separate space for a moment to allow us to cool off. One thing for sure is that every time I have ever spanked, yelled, grabbed their shirt, or got the "Vulcan" grip on my children in anger, I have regretted it, deeply. Then, instead of dealing with their bad behavior, we were now forced to deal with mine.

The truth is, although I do believe in spanking, I hate to do it and try to resort to it only when absolutely necessary. I have tried to adopt a rule that the spanking is a consequence of putting themselves or others in harm's way, or being willfully disobedient. When I spank, which I pray is not often necessary, I have asked God to help me to not do it in anger.

Psalm 94:12 says that *blessed is the man whom God chastens, and teaches him out of thy law, that God will give him rest from the days of adversity.* The word *chasten* means *to instruct, correct, reform, and to teach.* Hebrews 12:6 says *for whom the Lord loves, He chastens.* God chastens us because He loves us. In the same manner, we should also chasten and correct our children because we love them. Love is the essential ingredient for discipline.

My Aunt Sukey always taught the example of the Scripture found in Psalm 23, *thy rod and thy staff, they comfort me.* If we used the rod and the staff more like the Good Shepherd to lead, to guide, to keep out of harm's way, we would have less need for the rod on the backside.

Proverbs 10:13 does clearly say, *a rod is for the back of him who is void of understanding.* That would seem to define the criteria for spanking. If there is just no other way to get a child to understand your expectations and they are willfully, continually disobedient, then the Bible suggests this type of punishment. I know that the topic of corporal punishment may stir some heated controversy and debate, but those in favor may argue that when prayer, the ten commandments, and corporal punishment were allowed in schools, we didn't hear about children getting killed by one another.

Sometimes we as adults use just the threat of a spanking to get the obedience and response we are desiring from our children. I'm not saying that's right; I'm just saying we do it. I've heard things like "I'm gonna beat the fire out of you!" or "Let me get my belt," or "I'm going to whip you like there's no tomorrow." My husband's personal favorite is, "I'm gonna spank your hind end 'til it lights up like the Fourth of July!" to which my boys laugh hysterically, defeating the purpose of the whole threat.

My grandmother, who almost never got angry with us, would say from time to time when necessary, "Alright, go around the back of the house and bring me a hickory switch." She never once used it, but just the thought of my grandmother being disappointed in my behavior sure was effective. I don't think disciplining with threats and intimidation is recommended by the experts, but in my case as a child, it sometimes got my attention.

Job 36:10 says that God opens our ears to discipline. That means as mothers we have to be willing to hear God's instruction and discipline in order to be prepared to lead our children. If we as mothers are undisciplined or unteachable in any area, it is hard to instill teachable qualities in our children. If we moms are unyielding to the discipline God sends into our lives, how are we qualified to discipline someone else?

What I am finding to be more effective and necessary than threats of corporal punishment, is just plain old positive reinforcement and affirmation for the things they are doing well. "I like the way you are sharing with your friend." "I appreciate the way you swept the driveway with a good attitude." "I like the way you came to the dinner table the first time I called." "Wow, look what a great job you did cleaning your room!" "I know you can do it!" "Good job!" All day long I try as much as possible to shower my children with praise and affirmation. That way they are clear on the expectations of their behavior.

This doesn't mean I don't frequently blow it, especially when I am tired or stressed. The other day, I thought I was going to take one of my children's head off when he decided to pour green food coloring on our sofa. At that point you can bet I was thinking, "I like the way you are so creative with the food coloring!"

Another form of punishment we have learned in some of the parenting classes we've attended is in using consequences like denying a privilege such as TV time or grounding. This sometimes winds up being more painful for the parent than it is for the child. I can see you all shaking your head in disagreement on that one.

There's another form of discipline I frequently use when my children are fighting with one another. This idea was give to me by a mother from Toccoa, Georgia. She liked to call this form of discipline "nose to nose." When her children fought, she'd make them stand nose to nose until they burst into laughter and then were made to apologize to one another. This really does help to dispel arguments.

One last form of discipline I'd like to mention is in Truett Cathy's book[1]. He suggests that when younger children get unruly, sometimes what they need most is love and affection. It is for that reason, each one of his Chick-Fil-A corporate-sponsored boys' homes have rocking chairs for the house parents to hold and rock that little boy who continues to act out.

I once read a report on male prison inmates and the fact that an overwhelming majority of them never remember receiving any

---

1. S. Truett Cathy, *It Is Better to Build Boys than Mend Men* (Looking Glass Books, 2004).

empathy from their mothers when they were hurt or distressed. And they certainly did not remember being held or loved. Sometimes, moms, we can overdo the *be quiet, big boys or big girls don't cry* routine. We believe in a lot of affection and hugs in our family. And I think it brings a very healthy response.

As a mother, I hope I will open my ear to the discipline of God so that I can train my children to do the same. I'm sure no expert on the subject of discipline and I have much to learn. It is my hope that I will continue to stay open and pliable to the Holy Spirit in order to grow. My prayer is that I will be the kind of mother who will temper all discipline with love, respect and no anger. That's my prayer for you, too.

What are some areas God has been speaking to you about in regard to discipline in your own life?

____

____

____

____

____

Write a few areas you would like to change in regard to the disciplining of your children.

____

____

____

____

____

A Mother's Prayer

Father God, help me to have ears that listen and receive Your discipline in my own life. Help me to teach discipline and good judgment to my children. Make me into a strong role model in the area of discipline so that my children will see consistency and love in all that I do. Give me wisdom and strength to make the right choices on how to deal with each situation that arises with my children.

I ask You, Holy Spirit, to parent through me, as many times I feel I don't know what I am doing. Forgive me for when I have disciplined or spoken in anger to my children. And help them to forgive and not harbor resentment toward me for it. I speak a blessing over my children that they will be people of goodness, integrity, good character, and strength.

In Jesus' name I pray. Amen.

CHAPTER 18

THE MARVELOUS MADNESS OF GETTING GOD-TIME AND GIRL-TIME

...Forsaking not the assembling of ourselves together. Hebrews 10:25

Ah, finally some peace and quiet. I've waited a week for this. Edward took the children with him for lunch, giving me a few moments to be alone with the Lord and write. The sound of the house with no children is so quiet it is almost deafening. When I was just beginning to settle in, pray, and enjoy opportunity, a big, red, noisy tractor appears right outside the door. Back and forth, back and forth it goes on the lawn outside. So loud and distracting that I'm about to give up my efforts. I could swear he's cut the same mound of grass fifty times! From the look on his face, I can tell that the man on the tractor is totally enjoying himself. He looks like he thinks he's a kid on a roller coaster or something. "This is useless," I say in frustration. "I can't pray or write with all these distractions!"

As a mother, trying to find some quiet time with God can be challenging. Maintaining some personal space and time can be as painful as a root canal. Sometimes I think I'll just read my Bible in the bathroom. Just being able to go to the bathroom with privacy is a luxury. It never fails that I just get the door closed to the bathroom and have a seat, when all of a sudden comes a loud, shrill, "Mom! Where are you, Mommy? I need you!" Pretty soon there is another small person in the "water closet" with me and I am nervously hurrying to cater to his demands. Trying to go to the bathroom with someone hanging on your legs is quite challenging.

Being discreet with my bathroom time and all the, shall I say, "complications" we women endure has been taken to a whole new level with children. When they were really small, I made a point of trying to hide all feminine hygiene products, but to no avail. They would burst into the bathroom where I was, proudly handing one to me. Whenever they would see me going in with one in my hand, I would quickly plead, "Please, I need some privacy here!" This led them to believe that all feminine hygiene products are called "Privacies!"

"Mom, do you need a privacy?" my sons would ask in such a helpless tone.

"No, thank you!" I'd respond thinking to myself, *Now hurry and get out of here!*

Your mama won't tell you that when children are toddlers, it is rare for a mother to even get a shower in peace. Pretty soon, they're all in there with you, hogging the water! "Can Mommy rinse off now?" I ask while shivering in the corner.

Children use your hair products, your brush, your toothpaste, your towel and everything else because a mom's bathroom is so much more interesting than their own! "Can't a girl have a little something? Just a little peace? I mean, just a corner of the house that is hers?" I frequently hear myself asking. "Why does everyone have to mess up my stuff? Use your own!" (I'm sure y'all know what I'm talking about—especially the moms with girls!)

Just trying to maintain your own identity and not totally losing who you are as a woman is a tremendous feat in itself. Rather than being known for our name, we become known as our child's mother. "Oh, that's Davis' mom, what's-her-name," or "She belongs with Hamilton," people say. We ourselves tend to forget our own name and identity.

Just the other day, Truett had followed at my heels for several hours. Almost every five seconds, he would say, "Mom—Mom—Mom—Mom—Mom—Mom." It was beginning to have a jackhammer effect on my mind. I turned to him and said, "Truett, can you stop saying 'Mom' for five minutes? I need a break!"

He quickly replied, "Okay...Becky-Becky-Becky-Becky-Becky." Up until then I really didn't realize he even knew my name! *Oh yeah,* I thought. *My name is Becky! I have a name! I am an individual. I have wants and needs and dreams and plans, too!*

Looking in the mirror a few moments later, I said to myself, *"Mom, meet Becky."* I wondered who that really was looking back at me. Where did that young girl go? I mean, just the other day I was sixteen and carefree, spending hours alone in my room, listening to music, trying new hairstyles, putting together new outfits, dreaming about boys and such. Why, I had lots and lots of time alone! I never dreamed how much I would crave it later in life or that one day I'd have to make a speech to my children announcing in advance that I had to go to the bathroom and didn't want to be disturbed! Of course, when they are little, my speech just made them curious all the more.

Mothers and want-to-be mothers, let me tell you now: we have to fight for some time alone, time with God, and time with other Godly women. We have to educate the other people in our house about our need for "girl space." We have to insist upon some time alone to pray and to be with girlfriends. You know what I mean? Men do it all the time! "Honey, I'm playing golf today," or whatever the activity may be. Sometimes they don't even tell.... Now, I'm not suggesting that, but I am saying that a girl's gotta do—what a girl's gotta do!

Recently my friend heard the negativity getting worse and worse in my voice in our phone conversations as I relayed our latest saga.

"You're getting pretty negative, Becky," she would say straight up. "I'm getting concerned about you!" Aren't you thankful for those straight-up girlfriends? You have to have them in your life, someone to "jack" us up when it is needed.

One day she said, "I'm coming over this afternoon to see you! There's something I feel God wants me to do and I am going to do it!"

"Well, what is it?" I asked, thinking maybe with my bad attitude it had to do with intense deliverance or something.

"I'm not telling you," she said. "It's a surprise."

Being the control freak that I can be, I kind of fretted for the next several hours. Pretty soon, Shay, our sitter who I claim as my daughter, showed up at our house. A few moments later Debi arrived.

"I called your baby sitter to sit your children because we're going somewhere. You've been 'cooped up' in this house working, and I feel you need to get out and live a little!"

"Really?" I said happily. "Where are we going?"

"Just don't ask questions!" she said. "You'll see."

As we got into her van to leave, she handed me a new copy of what is now one of my favorite books which, if applied, would change my life. Next she said proudly, "We are going to have a pedicure. And then we are going to have coffee and talk!"

I was so excited I could barely breathe! She was right. I had gone much too long a time without getting out with a friend. I was long overdue for some "girl time."

What a wonderful and memorable afternoon we had. I shall never forget it as long as I live! Just what the doctor ordered. It was an incredibly thoughtful and unselfish display of friendship and love. But what was so special to me about that afternoon was that my friend took the time to really hear the desperation in my voice and recognize that I needed to get out—even when I didn't see it myself. Particularly humbling is the fact that she is the mother of four girls herself, having just had her fourth baby! What she had done for me, I should have been doing for her!

Edward has been known to say to me when he knows I've reached my limit, "Well, just get in the car and go somewhere! I'll stay with the children."

"Where am I going?" I'll retort. "To the grocery store?" I've even been known to say in the past, "There's no money to go shop for clothes!" Then how about, "The traffic is terrible at this time of day. Besides, it's too hot to go anywhere."

Translation please: In other words, I'd rather stay here, complain and make everyone else miserable. And you know that I am being as honest as it gets, girls. You know that feeling we get when presented with the chance to get away from the children and we don't know where to go!

The point is, in order to succeed through the marvelous madness of motherhood years, you have to schedule time for yourself and time to be with your girlfriends. And yes, I mean with no husband, no boyfriend, no dogs or cats, and definitely no children! We have to have this *girl space* or our motherhood won't be too marvelous!

It is for that reason that I rarely miss our weekly women's Bible study on Tuesdays. It is a saving grace! Childcare and everything! For one and half glorious hours, some of my most favorite women in the whole world and I spend time together listening to good teaching, studying the Word, sharing our hearts and lifting one another in prayer. It has become one of my favorite times of the week.

These women inspire me in so many ways! Every time I go—even when I don't feel like it—I leave with a desire to be a better Christian, a better wife, a better mother, a better daughter, a better sister, and a better friend. When I first started attending I was going through a bit of the doldrums. One of the things that these beautiful girls rekindled and inspired in me was a desire to "fix up" a bit, put on a little make-up, do my hair, wear high heels in the middle of the day for no reason, and celebrate being a woman.

"Well, that's not very spiritual," I hear some of you thinking. Maybe not to you, but it sure is to my husband! He loves it and it has done wonders for my marriage! And that's very spiritual! You see, living in a house full of men and testosterone can kind of make you forget your "girly-ness." These women have helped me to hang onto that. And I love them for it!

Our pastor's wife recently started "Girls' Night Out," giving women the opportunity to come together and just have fun. For those of you who may not see that as a ministry, just ask the single woman or the single mom who deals with loneliness and isolation, wanting the chance to just have fellowship. Just ask the young mom with a house full of small children. Just ask the widow. Just ask the woman who works all day. There are many women in our communities and churches who rarely have the chance to get together socially and just enjoy each other's company. Girls' Night Out reminds us as a church that it is important to meet the needs of the whole man or woman on our church pews.

You see, just like playing with our children, playing with our girlfriends is just as important. It takes an effort on our parts. It doesn't come naturally. For some of us, it could be easier to just stay at home and unload the dishwasher or lie on the couch and feel sorry for ourselves.

The thing about it is that whether you need to invest some time with God alone or invest some time in a girlfriend, it takes an investment. It takes T-I-M-E. In the midst of a noisy busy household, how does a mother have the opportunity to be alone with God? When can she find a few uninterrupted moments to read the Bible? The only answer, my dear sister, is to get up early and/or stay up late. Once I felt prompted by God to begin my day in the Bible and end it at night in the Bible. In that way, I am spending time hearing His voice. Sleep is a pretty precious commodity for a mother, but even more is time alone with God.

Train your children to respect your time with God and let them know when you need to go into your room, shut the door and hit your face in prayer. When they ask, "What are you doing, Mom?" you can say, "I'm spending time alone with God so I can be a better mom." It's as necessary as oxygen! God-time and girl-time, two essentials to being the marvelous mother God meant you to be!

Scripture says in Colossians 1:27, *Christ in me, the hope of glory.* That's the beautiful thing about spending time with women of God. You can be sure that Christ is IN them! When we fellowship together with other women of the faith, according to this Scripture, we are spending time with Christ. When you have done it to the least of these, you have done it to Him (See Matthew 25:40). Investing time, gifts, a phone call, a note, love, lunch, a pedicure, coffee, whatever with a sister in Christ is like doing something for Christ Himself. His Spirit is within us. There's no better friend than a friend in Christ!

Hebrews 10:25 tells us to *forsake not the assembling of yourselves together.* Fellowshipping and worshipping together were two important characteristics of the New Testament church. Being together to laugh, to play, to worship, to pray, to eat, to study and to celebrate are all vital and essential requirements for the body of Christ today.

So what about you, mom? Have you committed yourself to getting into God's presence? Are you committed to the assembling of yourself with other believers? If not, you're missing out!

When do you spend time alone with God?

____

____

____

____

Where is your special place where you like to go to spend time alone with God?

____

____

____

____

Who are some of the women of God you enjoy spending time with for fellowship?

____

____

____

____

What are some of the fun things you have done together?

____

____

____

____

____

____

____

If you can't answer the above question, we've got some dreaming to do. Begin here by planning some adventures with some Godly friends.

____

____

____

____

____

____

____

____

A Mother's Prayer

Father God, we thank You that in this chapter You have revealed to us all, writer included, the necessity of spending first, time alone with You, and also time with other women of God. Thank You that You made us a whole person—spirit, soul, and body—and that You desire for us to be healthy and balanced in all these areas. Help us to make time each day to be alone with You to hear Your voice. Help us not to neglect or forsake the assembling of ourselves together in fellowship with other women of God. Help us to realize that when we are spending time with other women of God, we are essentially spending time with Christ Himself. Teach us how to nurture our relationship with You and our relationship with others, that we would be better wives and mothers and, most of all, better ambassadors for Your kingdom.

In Jesus' name we pray. Amen.

CHAPTER 19

THE MARVELOUS MADNESS OF SCHOOL DAYS

He wakens me morning by morning, wakens my ear to listen like one being taught. Isaiah 50:4

It was such an emotional time for me when my first baby went off to kindergarten. I felt a sick feeling in the pit of my stomach and an ache in my heart as I had to leave him for the first time. Another more seasoned mom tried to console me by saying, "Becky, get used to it. You cry when the school year is over in the summer, and you cry when the school year begins."

Turning your child over to strangers to be surrounded by other strangers who are being raised by strangers is a pretty daunting thing. Not to mention the routine and the schedules and the homework and the fundraisers and the lunch money and the PTO meetings and the teacher conferences and the school rules and the school supplies and the dress codes and…we could go on and on.

Whether your children are starting school for the first time or are returning, remember that eventually you do get used to it. You get conditioned to the demands that school life puts on your kids and on the whole family. You begin to get a little wiser, I hope, with each passing year as to how best to handle the routine and make the process of getting ready for school as pleasant as possible. There are some tricks of the trade I have learned, and I am learning to implement them with my children. They seem to make life flow more smoothly.

One of those gems of wisdom I learned from the FlyLady. Yes, that's what I said! When I overheard several of my friends talking about her and the things they had learned on her website, FlyLady.net, I thought I should check her out. I hope you will, too. One of her biggest tips for women and mothers is to have a night-time routine every night. This is a "without even thinking" routine or habit that FlyLady encourages women to do that makes the start of each new day so much more enjoyable. Instead of rushing around in the mornings like crazy women in our dirty bathrobes, wild untamed hair and a messy house, FlyLady gives us solutions.

Instead of searching under couches for a match to a sock or debating with our children about whether they want peanut butter and jelly or turkey, we leisurely drink a cup of coffee and have our devotion time in peace while the children are getting dressed without a hitch. The secret to the FlyLady's "no fuss" morning is this: you simply do the hard things at night. You lay out the clothes, including shoes and socks. You prepare the lunches ahead of time and put them back into the refrigerator. The children empty out their backpacks, do their homework, and have necessary papers signed and put back in the folder—all the night before!

You finish the dinner dishes and clean your kitchen. And—the FlyLady's special—you shine your sink, each night! You make your coffee. You decide what needs to be laid out for breakfast. You and your children do a run through the house to pick up stray clothes, toys, towels and whatever else has cluttered your life. When this routine is completed, life becomes less stressful and your home a more pleasant place to live.

Where is the mom in the dirty bathrobe and messy hair? Why, she's putting on her shoes and her lipstick for the day! Having had her devotions, enjoyed a cup of coffee, made her bed, woken the children and poured their cereal for breakfast, she's able to dress and prepare mentally for the day.

Now, in a perfect world, this would be wonderful, right? Even I must admit that there are evenings when every ounce of energy has been completely squeezed from my soul, and I couldn't possibly think of ironing shirts for my children's school day or going to the kitchen to prepare lunches. But FlyLady's point is this: Learn to fly. Learn to take the little baby steps each day and do something in your nighttime routine so that your mornings are not so chaotic.

There are days, I will tell you, that when my children have left for school, I look around my home and the aftermath of it all—cereal all over the table, pajamas all over the family room where they *had* to change clothes in front of the TV, unmade beds, toys everywhere, and the remnants of the lunch fixins. It can be frightening, almost as if a storm blew through. What I am learning to do in baby steps is to do at least one or two things each night before school—even if it's just finding some socks. In this way, everyone's life should be just a little happier in the morning, and some of the madness has been taken from the routine.

Another fear or concern I frequently hear mothers talk about these days is with bullies. What about those school bullies? How dare they harass our sweet little babies, right? No matter how nice and wonderful your school may be, almost every school has a bully who will try to frustrate and intimidate your child. It may be at times our own children who are not being very kind to a classmate—imagine that!

I can remember in the fourth grade, I had my one and only experience with a bully in school. I will never forget her! For some reason which I don't recall, she took a strong disliking to me. Of course, it couldn't have been anything I said or did to her because I was a perfect little angel. Hmmm. But this girl along with two others decided to start before class in the morning the "We Hate Becky Club," complete with a chant and pounding on the desks as I entered the room, if the teacher wasn't present.

At first I tried to keep a stiff upper lip and not allow it to bother me. The more I ignored them, the louder they got. Then several days into this cruelty treatment, I broke. I simply couldn't take starting my day like that and being bullied by those three girls. I can remember going home that day and crying to my mother about the situation.

Being the wise woman that she was, what do you think she did? Did she storm up to the school and demand to see the teacher? Did she ask to see the principal? The school board? Did she call and threaten the bullies' families? Nope, in none of these ways did my mother respond. You know what my mother did? She did call the girl's mother. But it was not to even discuss the "We Hate Becky Club" that her daughter presided over. It was to invite her over to our house after school for cookies and some play time.

Wow! Looking back, what a mom! She did come over one afternoon and we wound up having a pretty fun time together. My mother showed her wonderful generous spirit of love and hospitality and shared maybe a few words to her that I shall never know or remember about being kind to one another. But this I do know. From that day forward, she resigned as president of the "We Hate Becky Club" and it disbanded.

Looking back on that incident has been a real source of guidance for me as my children have gone through not such dramatic, but slightly similar conflicts in school. I am so thankful for that example of love and turning the other cheek that my mother modeled for me that day. Things got easier for me and I was able to complete the fourth grade without an ulcer. Sometimes, really all a bully wants anyway is a little love and attention.

Another word of advice that I would like to share about school is this: Don't be motivated by guilt to volunteer for hours and hours of work at the school. If you take a job, whether it is room mom (which I served as for quite a few years) or a PTO office, do it because you feel God wants you to serve in that position. If you are called to that, and you have the time without taking away from your family, then great! Go for it! But if we have allowed those school projects to come before God, family, your husband, and especially even your children, you need to seek some balance. Sometimes we get so busy working *for* our children that we forget to have relationship *with* them. End of sermon. Just ask God to direct your involvement at school and He will bless your efforts.

My final thought about school is on how to survive the homework. If children have a set routine in the afternoon, such as snack time, homework, chores, and TV time or play time, it makes the afternoon more pleasant. On the days when I have allowed the children to come in and turn on the TV and eat, the homework doesn't get done sometimes 'til bedtime. Establish a routine that works best for you and your child and try your best to stick to it every day.

Bedtime routines are important in order for our children to get enough sleep and to prepare for the next day. During school in particular, children need extra sleep and parents need their sanity. We believe, like many of you, that ending the day with prayer over your children is important. Our children request it. (I'm writing this late at night as my oldest peeks out of his room for the third time in thirty minutes.)

As for the teacher who comes to you and says your child struggles on everything, will only be average, or maybe is having some behavior issues, my advice to you is this—as much as you can, always back the teacher, but you don't have to agree with every assessment of your child. The best thing to do is to try not to get into a major confrontation or disagreement with the teacher. Look, teachers have a hard enough job, and they are not compensated nearly enough for the hassles they endure. Let's give our teachers a break. But if we do encounter one who says some negative things about our child, pray about it rather than react to it.

One of my children had a wonderful teacher who made some comments about him to me that were most discouraging. She reported to me in front of my friend and her children that my child was struggling on some achievement tests and was the last to finish. She continued to comment that she feared he was only going to be able to work on an average grade level throughout school.

God gave me the grace to not respond at the time, but you can bet when I got home, I dug my heels in to pray. All this time, Edward and I have continued to pray and believe for him to succeed in school and not struggle. I am happy to report that five years later, my child has made mostly As and Bs and made the honor roll most every semester. But, even if he hadn't made honor roll and did struggle to make a C, does that make him less of a person? You know the answer to that! Absolutely not!

Cover your child in prayer every day. Speak a blessing over them before they leave your home. Pray over their focus, their behavior, their attitude, and their relationships. Ask God for favor with their teachers, principal, and other students. Bless their day to joy!

Oftentimes a child will have to leave a home where there was anger and strife. I've done it—we probably all have. How is a child supposed to function and focus when there is hell at home? The answer is, they can't. It is up to us to maintain a spirit of peace and joy and for our children to be sent off from a home of love, safety and security. Not blow-ups! It is difficult to choke down some breakfast in fear as anger erupts in the home before school. It's no way for us to send our children into the world they are facing today. They deserve better. They deserve a peaceful and secure start to their day.

Hopefully the few tips on surviving school will help you. Some of the best advice I have ever gotten from a mom was this: Stay engaged. Don't clue out with your children. Stay involved and interested and concerned. Know who their friends are. Eat lunch with them every now and then. Attend school functions. Know their teachers. A little effort goes a long way.

Someone recently relayed a story to me about an experience he had while taking children to school. He pulled up to the school, walked the children to their classes, and returned to the car to leave. As he did, a mother in a "monster truck" wheeled in right next to him, late. Although the window of his vehicle only met the top of her tire, he looked up to see this mother talking intently on her cell phone. She turned to the back of the truck to tell her daughter to get out. In a moment, he looked up to see this little girl struggling to get out of this huge truck with backpack and papers falling out and flying everywhere. Next he saw the little girl struggling to climb down the three-foot drop to the ground, trying to retrieve the papers and backpack from under the vehicle. All this was done while the mother continued to talk on the cell phone.

Hopefully this was not the scenario every morning for this little girl, but even still, my heart broke for her. I mean, come on, moms. Can't we turn off the dumb cell phone for five minutes to walk our child to class or to drop them off before they begin their day? Don't they deserve at least some eye contact and a hug or smile? I don't mean to preach here, but I think the world has gone cell phone crazy! I guess I had that to my advantage growing up. The closest thing to a cell phone was a CB radio, and my mom wouldn't have been caught dead talking on that as she dropped me off to school.

The point again is this: Stay engaged. Stay engaged with your children. Stay clued in to them for the moments, and I mean moments, that we spend together each day. These few moments are but mere glimpses in time that we have to pour into them seeds of love that someday will bloom and blossom in their lives.

Write some specific goals to better engage with your children.

At home:

____

____

____

____

At school:

____

____

____

____

At church:

____

____

____

____

A Mother's Prayer

Father God, protect my children as they grow and go off to school. Surround them at all times as a shield. Place them in the very classes and situations You want them in. Remove any evil persons or teachers from their presence. Hold them in the palm of Your hand. Surround and cover their schools, classes, teachers, and classmates with the blood of Jesus. Allow them to bloom and blossom in the place where You plant them.

Holy Spirit, I ask You to accompany them in their classes, in the hallways, in the cafeteria, in the car, or wherever they might be. Protect their minds from any untruths or confusion. We entrust our children to Your care and covering.

In Jesus' name we pray. Amen.

CHAPTER 20

THE MARVELOUS MADNESS OF SPORTS AND CHILDREN

Wherefore seeing we also are compassed about with so great a cloud of witnesses, Let us lay aside every weight, and the sin which doth so easily beset us, and let us run with patience the race that is set before us.... Hebrews 12:1

With a house full of kids, sports become a part of your life. We've participated in most of the organized sports, with the exception of soccer, because my children never expressed a desire to play, even when we encouraged them to do so. We've played lots of golf, basketball, softball, football, and karate. With each sport comes a different dynamic of lessons learned, for both the children and the parent.

Edward and I have been quite involved with some of the sports like basketball and football, helping with the coaching and team parents. We've enjoyed lots of Saturdays cheering for our boys on the basketball court and watching our kids grow and excel right before our eyes. We've usually been some of the loudest parents on the sidelines to root for our kids. Our boys have never been the biggest or the fastest or the most skilled on their teams. Thus far, they haven't been the highest scorers or most valuable players.

Regardless, we cheer loudly because of their personal achievement. The achievement of having the courage to play in front of loud obnoxious parents, of showing up for practice, of listening to their coaches, of taking the shot or running the play. These are the accomplishments that really matter, not whether or not they are the next Michael Jordan. As a woman of God, I am certain Michael's mother, Mrs. Jordan, would agree that character development is first and foremost in importance when it comes to sports participation.

One of the many disciplines a child learns from participating in sports is learning to be at practice and games on time, prepared to participate. I can remember many practices, driving in on two wheels to get there on time. Not missing practice gives the child a sense of knowing that the rest of the team is counting on him to show up. That's the way it is in life. No one really is independent of one another. We are all somehow interconnected and dependent in some way on one another. Having the courtesy of showing up on time teaches a child responsibility and character.

Participating in Upward Basketball has been one of the highlights of our children's experiences. It is a church-based, Christian sports program for boys and girls which teaches them fundamentals of the sport with great spiritual and character building concepts. The team prays before each game and half time is given to a guest speaker who shares their faith in Christ. Upward programs are found in churches all over the United States, reaching grades K-6. We have so many fond memories of Upward with family and friends. My middle son's coach drove two hours one way to participate in the program we were involved with in our city. It is well worth the trip. To find out more about Upward, visit www.upward.com.

One of our happiest memories with children's sports was with my son's school flag football team, coached by my husband and a young man from our church. Our team was down ten points, but came back to win the game in the very last second when our quarterback threw to the receiver in the end zone and he caught the ball. It was a great victory against a team who was older and bigger than ours and had been undefeated the previous year. What a thrill it was for us all when we won! Players, cheerleaders, parents, grandparents, siblings, and teachers all rushed down the field to the end zone after the winning catch. It was a memory we will *never* forget! Probably a good thing there was no goal post for us to tear down!

Participating in their sports experience, cheering them on or assisting with coaching is an excellent way to stay engaged with your children. You can see clearly on the field or court their accomplishments, their challenges, and their fears. One parent said to me years ago, "Keep your children busy, not too busy, but keep them involved." Sports, school, and church activities channel a child's activity away from destruction and mischief and television to fun and achievement.

That great fall afternoon when we all rushed the end zone to celebrate and cheer our winning football team will forever be in our hearts and minds. The Scripture in Hebrews 12:1 reminds us that there is also a great cloud of witnesses in heaven who cheer with great enthusiasm and expectancy as they watch the events of our life unfold. They celebrate the victories God gives us and the hurdles we complete as we run with patience the race set before us in life. It would be great to remind ourselves and our children that there are cheerleaders in heaven, watching and waiting for us to fulfill the call of God on our lives. Our children's participation in sports here on earth should be toward that end of developing the God-character within and becoming the men and women God would have us all to be.

List some sports activities you would like your child to try.

____

____

Write some things your child has gained by participating in sports activities.

____

____

____

____

A Mother's Prayer

Father God, we give You praise for the plans and purposes You have set for our children. We thank You that You have a divine destiny for their lives. We thank You for the opportunities you give them to develop character and skills through participation in sports and other activities. Father God, I ask You to develop my children to their greatest potential and help them to be the best they can possibly be to bring glory and honor to You.

Father, I ask You that they will be victorious in their achievements and be the head and not the tail. I ask that You will give them divine favor and blessing in all they set their hands to do. Help them to be leaders and to influence and win others to Jesus Christ through Godly character at all times. Help them to remember that there is a great cloud of witnesses watching and cheering them on in heaven to be all they can be.

In Jesus' name I pray. Amen.

CHAPTER 21

THE MARVELOUS MADNESS OF BEING A SPIRITUAL MOTHER

> *Sing, O barren woman, you who never bore a child; burst into song, shout for joy, you who were never in labor; because more are the children of the desolate woman than of her who has a husband.* Isaiah 54:1

I will never forget the day I met my spiritual mother. A friend had taken me to her home in hopes that I would get the deliverance and ministry I so desperately needed at that time. The woman I affectionately called Mimi for twenty-three years, was sitting at her breakfast table with a cup of tea and her Bible open to a particular passage when I first met her in 1982. Little did I know that with this encounter, my life was about to change drastically forever.

She was a petite, beautiful redhead with a complete holiness about her demeanor. Dismissing a lot of formal introductions, Mimi began to read a Scripture from the Word of God that shot like an arrow straight to my heart. I took a seat next to her at the table and began to cry. Without knowing me at all, she had allowed the Holy Spirit to direct her to the very Scripture that would nail my circumstances. Her ability to operate with the gift of knowledge and discernment is profound.

Whatever it took to get me free and to stay that way, Mimi has done. She invited me to prayer meetings where other women of faith prayed for me. There, she washed my feet. At one time, she poured a whole bottle of oil on my head. She allowed me to be with her as she ministered to other people and taught me how to pray for them. She took me with her to what I now know were "historical" meetings, like with Dr. Ken Hagin. Many times, she took me out to eat with friends and family. One time she took me shopping for clothes. She allowed me to visit with her and her family for hours on end and became my family when I needed one. (And I know they all had to get tired of me being around.) Her own daughters and grandchildren just took me in and loved me like part of their family. For this I will always be grateful and never forget.

She would make a cup of tea for me and sit and listen as I talked. Once I had a 104-degree fever and was so sick I was hallucinating. She and some other prayer warriors came to my apartment and prayed over me 'til the fever broke. She flew to Georgia twice to minister to my friends and family there. She prayed for my future husband, Edward. She has prayed over me when I was pregnant and in labor. She has prayed over the phone for my boys countless times. She has prayed for me every time I have moved. She has prayed me through extreme times of darkness and depression. She has taught me things about the Lord that are invaluable and that have made me a completely new individual. And although at one point we lost contact with one another, not seeing each other in years, we speak on the phone several times each month. She remains a great source of comfort and guidance in my life.

How can you put a value on a spiritual mom? How can you begin to describe just how much someone like that means in a believer's life? She is a treasure that God dropped in my life, and at forty-something, I am just beginning to understand how incredibly blessed I am to have known her.

Since that day, she became to me a spiritual mother who has prayed and discipled me for over twenty years. She has ministered to hundreds and hundreds over the years and has taught them how to pray and hear the voice of God. While I know many others consider her a spiritual mother, she has a way about her of making you feel that you are the most important person in the world. There are so many spiritual principles that she has helped me to practice in my life, like learning to get quiet and wait on the Lord to answer. She has so accurately heard from the Lord words of knowledge that have been passed on to ministers who preached on that word to tens of thousands to see deliverance in their lives. She is an amazing woman of God. Not unfamiliar herself with many trials and tribulations, she continues ministering to ministers to build the body of Christ.

Titus 2 speaks of an older woman who is to train up the younger women in the church to be strong in faith. Where are the Titus 2 women of God today? If you are remaining silent and dormant in your gifts to the young women in the body, we ask you to rise up. We would petition you to speak up. We would encourage you to show up. Reach out your hands to the younger generation who are many times so void of training and knowledge of the Word that they are floundering in their walk with Christ.

I would say to the younger generation, open your heart and your eyes to the *imperative* need for spiritual mothers in your life who can pray you through the attacks of the enemy and the challenges of life. We need one another!

If we're not careful, we can segregate the older from the younger and miss out on so much rich interaction. There are, of course, times when it is appropriate to gather with women in our own age bracket, but to exclude one another as if one group is not relevant to the other is neglecting what we are told to do in Titus 2.

Titus 2 clearly says to *bid* the older women to do five things. *Bid* means to speak, tell, utter, set the discourse. Sometimes the younger woman needs to draw the wisdom out of the older. We are to BID them. What are the five things Titus tells us to do?

1. **Be reverent and devout.** The Living Bible translation says this means to be quiet and respectful, to be gentle in our approach.

2. **Engage in a sacred service.** Anything we do in the church is a sacred service whether it is cleaning, keeping the nursery, singing in the choir, praying—it is all about sacred service.

3. **Don't slander.** Slandering is a form of lying, gossip, judging. It is sowing discord (strife) among the brethren. Proverbs 6 states the six things that the Lord hates, and one is sowing discord among the brethren.

4. **Don't be slaves to drink.** In other words, don't be slaves to addictions. Addictions can be drugs and alcohol, but it can also be food, TV, shopping, entertainment, or any other source of escape.

5. **Give good counsel.** This means give counsel that can be backed up in the Word of God. It must be Biblical counsel. There are lots of counselors out there, but only those who offer the answers from the Word of God are effective. Life is in the Word of God.

These are the five requirements for the older women in our churches today. Think what a difference our older women could make if each young woman had at least one older woman who poured good, Godly, Biblical counsel into our hearts.

Titus 2 goes on to say that the older women are to live by these five standards, SO THAT…I have those words circled in my Bible because they are pivotal words. Why? Older women, do these five things in your life, SO THAT you can **train**. Notice that the word *train* is used here instead of another like *teach* or even *bid* in the previous verses addressing older women. Training is different from teaching. It means *provision, the "how to do" something, preparation, plan, rehearsal, foundation, and scaffolding*. The word *train* also does incorporate teaching, but it means *to get in the trench with the younger woman and rub elbows*. It means inviting the younger woman into your home and teaching them by showing them, and sometimes that gets messy.

I like to give the example of my children learning to cook. They always want to cook with eggs and it is a big deal to get to crack them. Now I could sit on the couch and yell instructions to my children on how to crack the egg, which would result in a huge mess and probably a lot of shell in the mixture. Or, I could get off my "blessed assurance," stand next to my children in the kitchen, and help them while they crack the eggs. Maybe it would be less messy, but it would require more effort on my part. That's called training.

Now let's take a look at what we are to train the younger women to do. There is a list of ten things.

1. Be sane. We live in a crazy world and we need older women to train us to be quiet and live peacefully, not freaking out and losing our sanity with every turn in life. We live in the noisiest society and generation in the history of mankind. To find peace and be peaceful is the challenge we all have to teach and encourage.

2. Be sober of mind. I saw a TV program where young mothers met weekly for a mom's night out at a local restaurant and would drink until they were completely drunk. Then some of the girls would drive themselves home. It was an incredibly sad situation. They all couldn't wait for their next gathering.

Maybe those of us in the body of Christ don't have the challenges with addictions to drugs and alcohol as some do, but what about addictions to food, shopping, TV, and other vices? A friend of mine once had a hat that read, "Shop 'til you drop." Now, what exactly does that mean? Shop 'til you just pass out? And how is that any different from the young mothers and their mom's night out, who drink 'til they pass out? Sober of mind means that we keep our mind focused and steadfast on the walk that Christ has set before us, not looking to the right or the left, but keeping in our sight the goal and prize of the high calling of Christ.

3. Love their husbands. It takes a strong older woman at times to reach out to the younger and encourage her to love unconditionally and stay with a situation when it looks like there is no hope. If it weren't for some older women in my life reminding me that marriage is to the death, I might have made a huge mistake. Living amid a divorce culture, we have to be trained how to love our husbands because, believe me, the honeymoon does wear off and the real love begins.

4. Love their children. There have been times when I was so exasperated with my children I could have lost it, literally. Loving our children has got to be unconditional. We must love them when they are loveable and when they are not, love them enough to tell them "no" and to discipline them, love them at times with tough love. Let's face it, there are really no manuals that come with our children at birth. So much of our parenting is by trial and error…in my case, more errors! It helps to have an older woman come alongside to train and assist in rearing children. Younger women, don't be so self-reliant that you miss receiving some wisdom and training from someone who has been there.

5. Self-controlled. To be self-controlled means able to control one's actions, not freaking out, flipping out, or going over the edge. It means controlled in every area of our life—in our speech, in our relationships, in our eating, in our shopping. That means no shopping 'til we drop! Developing the fruit of self-control is one of the most important and valuable fruits of the Holy Spirit.

6. Chaste. The actual meaning of *chaste* is *to be clean-minded, to censor what you put in your mind.* There are lots of opportunities for moms to sit at home and fill our minds with things that are not chaste. Daytime TV is flooded with soap operas and talk shows that are full of the sensual, unclean, and ungodly counsel. Don't tune in to that junk!

7. Homemakers. Teaching the art of homemaking has become something you don't hear as much about anymore. The attack on the home has been hell's greatest effort in the last three decades. Learning how to manage and run a home is one of the most noble things a woman and a man can learn. Running a household is much like running a business. There are financial, social, emotional, and practical challenges to learn.

Homemaking is a ministry to your family. Cooking a meal and serving it hot is a ministry. Homemaking is a skill that has to be developed over time and must begin being taught as a girl is growing up. If you are a young woman, praying for a husband and a family one day, one of the best things you can do is to find a Proverbs 31 woman in your church or in your family and learn from her. Glean everything you can on how to run an orderly home.

Good-natured and kindhearted. Here's an area that is a weakness for me. I have a tendency to be a little on the negative side and when things don't go my way in my home, I can quickly develop a bad attitude. I have no problem being kindhearted at church or in ministry, but when it comes to being kindhearted to my husband and children, sometimes I fall short. One of the things I have learned through the years is that as a woman, I am the spiritual and emotional barometer in my home. That old saying, "If mama ain't happy, ain't nobody happy" is so very true! When we get down or irritated, the whole household is affected. Training women how to not let our emotions rule us and thus rule our marriage and home is vital. If we could just learn to be the happiest in our home and the kindest in our home, what a wonderful life we would have. If we learned to be kinder to our husband than we are to anyone else, our marriages would truly be as days of heaven on earth. Train the young women to be good-natured and kindhearted—upbeat and positive about life, our children, our marriages and our homes.

Adapting to their husband. First Peter chapter three says also that women should adapt themselves to their husbands, which means to adjust to a specified use or situation. This means that we need to adapt ourselves and be in submission to our husband and the calling of God that is on their lives. A very wise woman recently reminded me that God did not bring me out of my husband's heart, mind, limbs, or any other place, but from his side. Woman was taken and formed from the rib of a man in his side. That means we walk side by side, co-joined in a mission for God together. It also means that we need to adapt to them physically, emotionally, financially, and socially. WE must learn to harmonize and flow together. Amos 3:3 says, *How can two walk together lest they be agreed.* When people are out of harmony, especially a married couple, a horrible sound comes forth. But when two people have adapted themselves to one another to harmonize—we can make a symphony.

Be in subjection to your husband. The word *subjection* can downright scare some women because it implies obedience. To be in subjection to a king or a ruler required loyalty and obedience to that headship. In the same way, God requires this subjection in a marriage relationship. Many of us when we are married repeat a vow which says *to love and obey.* In many recent years, I have noticed that couples take the word *obey* out completely, citing they are opting for a more contemporary version of the wedding vows. What I have found in my marriage is that without the critical element of obedience to Christ and obedience to our husbands, we have a surefire recipe for a disastrous failed marriage awaiting us. Titus 2 says that older women are to teach the younger women that there is nothing degrading about being in subjection to and obeying your husbands. There is safety in that obedience.

Recently I read a book on the subject in which the author pointed out that obedience is a crucifixion of our flesh and is not easy, even with the Godliness of husbands. But when you walk through a season where the husband is not living for God or is not making Godly decisions, the price of obedience can be painful. Of course, I do not mean compromising our own faith in any way or living immorally. But here's the point of the book: When we trust God and continue to honor, obey and be in subjection to our spouse, God will honor us and protect us and our children through the crisis.

Subjection is not something that comes naturally. That's why Titus reminded us as women to teach this, to model this, to develop this for the younger women in the body of Christ. When we honor God's command to honor and obey our husbands, God goes to work on our behalf and begins to bring order out of chaos and to set things right.

So that...

Titus 2 finishes by saying that all this is to be done *so that* the Word of God will not be blasphemed. In other words, women, we have to live it out. Our lives need to be living epistles read of all men.

We must live out the Word of God or we make it of no effect; it is blasphemed. When we sit in our churches today and receive the quality of teaching, preaching and study of the Word of God, but don't model it and live it in our marriages and homes, we blaspheme God.

So women, we must hold one another accountable for how we treat our families and husbands. Encourage one another to live out what we study and proclaim. Let us be authentic representatives of Christ, not perfect, but striving to live learning the Word.

The enemy would like nothing more than to silence the voice of the older women in our churches. He would like to make them feel as if their voices, their experience, their wisdom is not needed. He would want them devalued and relegated to nice little social gatherings. But Titus 2 says that we need spiritual mothers and their wisdom passed down to the younger. It is critical. It is a critical time in the body of Christ, and we must continue to teach Titus 2 and the Lord's return.

Identify some of the younger women in your life that you feel God prompting you to encourage or disciple.

____

____

____

____

Identify some of the older women in your life that you feel God prompting you to spend time with and glean from.

____

____

____

____

A Mother's Prayer

Father God, thank You for the lessons You have taught us in Titus 2. Thank You for the women You have placed in my life to be those Titus 2 women. Thank You, Lord, for the spiritual mothers You give us to help us grow into the women and mothers You have called us to be. Give me a fresh teachable spirit and a heart that remains open to the touch of Your Holy Spirit through Godly women in my life. Give me the ability to train those younger women You bring into my life and to spend quality time with them to pour into their lives as women have poured into mine. Help me not to be selfish with my home, my family, my children, my time and to allow others to be blessed by spending moments with us. May my life be an example of Your love and authenticity, not phoniness or fake Christianity. God, I want to be the real deal!

In Jesus' name I pray. Amen.

CONCLUSION

Now there stood by the cross of Jesus, his mother... John 19:25

The other day a little package arrived in the mail from my mother. I opened the envelope to find a small washcloth I had left at her house in Georgia a few weeks before. I told her if she found the cloth to keep it and use it. But being my mother, she lovingly wrapped it up along with a special note inside, and sent it to Phoenix. After opening it, my son Davis and I stood in the kitchen smelling it for a good five minutes to get the scent of my mother. There we were, passing it back and forth unashamedly as we held the cloth to our face. "Mmm, smells like Grandmama," Davis said.

I just adore my mother. Bernice Culbreth Davis has been one of God's greatest blessings and treasures in my life. You know I adore you, too, Dad, but this has been a book about motherhood. And I say this with great trepidation and sensitivity to those of you who don't have those same feelings toward your mother or maybe have lost your mother to death. But for these closing moments together, I ask you to hear me out as we apply these lessons to our own motherhood.

I adore my mother for so many reasons. I adore her beauty and grace. I adore the fact that she's gotten even more beautiful with the years. I adore her great spiritual wisdom and insight and that she so freely shares with me. I adore her as a grandmother to my children. I adore the poems she has written for each of her grandchildren on their first birthday, and for how she sneaks to feed them cake and icing when they are small babies. I adore her handwritten letters and thoughtful notes. I adore her laughter and lighthearted ways. I adore how she allowed me the freedom when I was growing up to ride my bike with my friends to the store to buy a sack of candy. And I adore how she sat beside the pond to watch for the alligator. I adore our two-hour telephone conversations on Sunday afternoon. I adore her love and devotion to my father. I adore her southern cooking. I adore her ability to make any home neat and beautiful. And I adore the way she has prayed for me and poured into my life and loves the Lord more than anything, making this book possible. And on and on I could go.

Yes, she and I have had a few ups and downs through the years. And she would attest to the fact that we have rubbed one another the wrong way, my being the primary irritant. There have been a few years in the past of relational distance between us, I am sad to say. But what I am discovering as I get older is the incredible blessing of motherhood and the unmistakable impact a Godly mother can make on the life of her children.

For some of us, appreciating our mothers as we should takes time, and for others of us it takes not having her close. My, how I have learned that lesson living thousands of miles from her physical presence. It gets harder and harder to say goodbye when we leave her. It gets harder to say goodbye to my husband's mother, who I adore as well. What a beautiful example of love she has been as she has given many years of caring for her own mother who is now ninety-two. You inspire me!

In a recent small group discussion at our women's Bible study, we began talking about the need and importance of spiritual mothers in our church. One of my dear friends and mentors said to me, "I believe that the reason you have a strong desire and willingness to receive from those who are older, Becky, is because of the fact that your mother has poured into you spiritually."

Hmmm, I thought to myself. That's a good thing for me to keep in mind in regard to my own children and in navigating this marvelous maddening experience we call motherhood. I may be learning such wonderful and fantastic things in Bible study or in church, but if I am not spoon-feeding these truths back to my children, I am missing one of my first callings in life.

In John 19:25 we read where Mary sat beside the cross of Jesus. She sat there sharing the pain. That's the thing about a Godly mother. A Godly mother will sit by your cross and bear your pain. A Godly mother will keep watch when we are in the valley of the shadow of death, and she will pray. The heritage of a mother who loves and serves God is perhaps the greatest blessing of life. A Godly mother will refuse to leave your side (spiritually) during your darkest hour. This still, another reason I adore my mother.

Maybe you are one of those precious moms who is reading this and thinking, *Well, Becky, I didn't have a Godly heritage. I've never had the unwavering support of my mother. She's never sat beside the crosses of my life. I don't have happy memories of my mother.* Maybe this has been a great source of sadness in your life. Perhaps this conversation has stirred some tender emotions. If you were here with me now, I would want to put my arms around you and love you. I would want to say that I am sorry for the pain. Better still, Jesus Himself wants to put His arms around you and take the pain away. He will do it if you ask Him.

Perhaps the greatest lesson of this book on motherhood is in the need for more Godly mothers in this world. We need strong women of the Word who can come alongside to say, "You can make it!"

As I close, I wince at the thought of all the aspects of motherhood that I have not addressed. There is so much more than what we have discussed on these pages, so much more that I have yet to experience in my own life and in my children's lives. There are things like the marvelous madness of teenage years—which I'm just getting a taste of now! Then there are the marvelous or maddening aspects of motherhood like babysitters, birthday parties, sleepovers, play dates and working outside the home. I have some good stories about some of those, as I'm sure you do, too!

The more I wrote on this subject of motherhood, the more I realized what a marvelous and complex calling it really is. Just remember that the next time someone asks what you do and you are tempted to say, "I'm just a mom." I know this thing called motherhood can be maddening, but with Christ, it becomes marvelous. He teaches you by His Spirit to take mental snapshots of your children along the way and to treasure every moment. There really is no other way to live your life with true joy and peace than to live with Jesus.

Maybe you have been reading this book and you are saying in your heart, "Becky, I want to be that Godly mother that you have been talking about. I want to leave a legacy of faith and hope for my family. I need to be healed of bad memories with my own mother. I need to ask forgiveness for my own blunders and mistakes. I want my children to remember me for the good things of God I have poured into their lives. How can I be that kind of mother?"

Well, I have the answer, and His name is Jesus. The place I will take you to is the place where we found His own mother Mary—at the foot of the cross. If you have never asked Him into your heart to be your Lord and Savior, there's no better time than now. Pray along with me out loud!

Father God, I ask You to come into my heart. Forgive me of my sins. I repent for living my life without You. Heal me of all past hurts and resentments. Forgive me of trying to live my life as a mother without You. Fill me with Your Holy Spirit and teach me to be the mother You have called me to be.

In Jesus' name I pray. Amen.

I pray that this book has brought laughter, healing and reflection. I pray that it has been a healing oil poured out on a weary mom's soul and that you found comfort in the pages. Most of all, I pray that the message here has taken you into God's presence, the place where troubles vanish and hearts are mended. May you be blessed in your endeavors to be a Godly mother and may God lead you and guide you in all that you do!

Blessings!

Becky Keener

ABOUT THE AUTHOR

Rebecca Keener's passion for encouraging women to be all that God created them to be is evident in her easy-to-love Southern style of bringing God's truths to our everyday lives. She has been a frequent Bible teacher at the women's meeting at Phoenix First Assembly of God and speaker at the Annual Phoenix Girls' Women's Conference.

Rebecca holds a Bachelor of Arts degree in Communications from Oral Roberts University. She has worked as a Marketing/Public Relations Director of two hospitals and as a trainer to corporations nationwide.

Rebecca and her husband Edward have been married for nineteen years and have three children. For the last eighteen years they have been active in church ministry as laypersons, being involved in marriage ministry, homeless outreach, children's, and women's ministry.

Rebecca Keener
Pleasant Place Farms
PO Box 527
Tiger, GA 30576
www.rebeccakeener.com

Psalm 16:6